PRAISE FOR THE WEAL

"I've witnessed many leaders, but I've never seen someone craft such powerful, unforgettable brands for women speakers as Ally Kennedy."

—Dr. Kevin Daley, Former Harlem Globetrotter, Award-Winning Speaker & Author

"She did a really good job of merging both mindset & tactics together. She left our audience feeling inspired, yet also capable of implementing big principles... Ally has a great stage presence, charisma, she definitely left the room feeling energized & uplifted."

—Jaden Easton, Co-Founder of Clients & Community

"Ally Kennedy is the Beyonce of branding for the stage. She's the founder of Six-Figure Speaker and, when you decide to start doing your own live speaking events and conferences, she's the one to go to for consulting on how to build it."

—Kimberly Spencer, Founder of Communication Queens

"From the moment I saw Ally share her message online I was hooked. There was something about the way she worded her communication that really pulled me in. It spoke directly to the things that light me up. It was about owning your power, claiming the stage, and closing high-ticket with confidence. Things I know a lot about. But she just had an energy to her and I felt strongly—"I need to know this woman".

I can tell we are "cut from the same cloth", inspired by the same things and trained in many of the same skills. But there was more. She said the things I wanted to say. Ideas about core desires to own the spotlight and be a category leader that I was still playing small around. She made me see that I can be even bolder and more authentic in my messaging and branding. I've been in the coaching game for 15 years and I've helped thousands of clients and spoken on stage with many of the top leaders and I think my message and skill set is pretty top notch. But after hearing Ally speak and then becoming friends and colleagues with her, I realize that she tapped into something that the world needs now and I'm thrilled to be a part of it... collaborating with her and rocking stages with her. Ally is a powerhouse and someone that I absolutely know, is on path to change a lot of lives."

—Sean D Stewart, FounderRock your Gift

"Ally is the embodiment of a relentless leader—her dedication to empowering women to share their unique messages and step into their true power is unmatched. I've had the privilege of working closely with her, and her impact on my own journey as a speaker has been nothing short of transformative. Ally has an extraordinary gift for seeing the depths of someone's story and revealing every powerful facet of who they are, guiding them to show up fully as the leader they're meant to be. This book is more than just a guide; it's an invitation to see yourself through the lens of Ally's wisdom. Her message has the power to reshape how you see your own potential and help you step boldly into the role of a true leader and how to share your message with millions who will be deeply moved by it. If you're ready to tap into your innate strength, gifts, and vision and make an impact that leaves a lasting legacy, let Ally's words be the guiding light on your journey."

—Stephanie Ann Swail, Founder of Soul Study & Relentless Leader

"Ally Kennedy is a powerhouse and this book gives the reader a glimpse into her genius mind. This book is for any woman who knows she is meant for more and wants to step into her power as a speaker and change the lives of others. The stories of success and lives changed in this book are incredibly impactful. You can tell how Ally has helped so many women create their own future and their own wealth including me. Ally helped me create the Empowered Women's Leadership Conference in the summer of 2024. The conference would not have been as successful or impactful if not for her guidance, direction, and passion. I am forever grateful for her belief in me and my event. The systems she lays out in this book will change the way you see yourself as a woman and an entrepreneur. I am grateful that Ally shared her book with all of us so that we can all benefit from her creative genius."

—Dr. Donna Marie Cozine, Founder, Sister Leader

"If you're considering hiring Ally, get ready for someone who wants to be involved, someone who cares about the outcome... this is someone who really cares about your success, your brand, what's good for the audience, what's good for the long term... this is someone who's really passionate about her craft, and she's a pro. You should definitely hire her if you think it's a good idea to show up as a pro yourself."

—Amanda Kauffman, Founder of The Coach's Plaza

"There is nobody like Ally in the industry. The way this woman's brain operates is on an entirely different level. She sees connections and can thread and weave stories in a way I have never seen before. I feel so lucky to have found her and the way I show up as a leader & CEO is completely different as a result! I am so lucky!"

—Hannah Rose Cluley, Founder, The Overflow Tapping Method for Coaches

"In the simplest terms: A force to be reckoned with. Her presence alone has the power to change your life. She walks in a room & you just wanna stand a little straighter & go a little deeper because she SEES you... She sees you but also brings that out of you."

—Irene Veronica, Business & Leadership Mentor

"Ally Kennedy is powerful! She is a natural born leader. When she hits the stage, she has the ability to capture the audience's attention and keep them engaged. As a mentor in the industry, she leads the masses to success. It was a pleasure attending her Wealthy Women Summit and I continue to be inspired by her fortitude to push forward. Adding Author to her title is remarkable and I'm so proud of her accomplishments."

—Janine Hernandez, Founder of the Book Publishing Academy

"Ally Kennedy is a bold, sexy, vibrant woman who captivates my desire to be seen and to be heard. She makes me feel safe to be me exactly as I am. My first experience with her was as a mentor and I knew immediately she possessed an incredible ability to collapse time. She was able to take the thoughts in my mind, the experience I have gained, and the knowledge I wish to share with my audience, and help me create an entire program in just a few hours! I've never seen anything like it. If you want to step into your power both as a woman and a leader then make sure you grab this book and grab a seat at her table. I am grateful for her belief in me and my abilities as a leader in my industry as a speaker and a speakers coach.

Every strong leader needs a powerhouse mentor to guide them along the way and keep you focused. Ally showed me just how easy it was to show up and be seen!"

—Roksana Zaya, Founder of Speakers Mastery &
The Light Therapy Lounge

"Being a part of the mastermind container, I was invited to be a guest expert at the Wealthy Woman Live Event and a Keynote Speaker at the Wealthy Woman Summit. Both of these opportunities were such an impactful platform for me to really gain notoriety in the industry and position myself as a go to authority in Human Design. I'm so grateful to Ally for building the stage for me!

Being in the mastermind itself, I have learned so much about myself, about my business, and about marketing, branding, strategy, systems, & foundations for business. I love the hybrid experience of having both a mastermind group but also 1:1 time with Ally herself. This is the first group experience where I've felt like my mentor is really hands on with me and truly has her eyes on my business. It's only been a few months and already I am seeing massive growth and momentum, attracting new clients, making sales, and finding my voice throughout it all. This whole experience has been empowering, the energy and support inside of Ally's containers are incomparable and so incredibly valuable.

Ally is a visionary and an innovator, she has the ability to see the big picture possibilities for your business and has the knowledge & capability to help lead you there. If anyone is considering jumping in to work with Ally, my advice is to GO FOR IT!"

—Jenna Garagiola, Founder, Soulful CEO

"Some women are born to disrupt the status quo and reshape the world. Ally is one of those women. She possesses a relentless fire, a mission to carve out a space where Wealthy Women can thrive in their authenticity.

I met Ally during a sales and marketing program, at a time when we were both reimagining our brands, programs, and identities. I watched her claim her authority when she created the Wealthy Woman brand, and I wanted to be in her sphere of influence so I could level up as well. She invited me to speak on stage at a Wealthy Woman Live event, and being in the arena ignited something in me that pushed me to step into my power as a speaker. Ally has a way of making women know they were meant for greatness."

—**Lilly Penhall, Founder, Penhall Publishing**

"True leadership goes beyond guiding others—it's about igniting a vision that empowers communities. Ally Kennedy embodies this rare kind of leadership. Through her unparalleled drive and the Wealthy Woman Live movement, she's not only built a program that uplifts women; she's crafted a global movement that encourages them to step boldly into their power, redefine their potential, and make meaningful strides toward financial independence and influence. Ally isn't just shaping leaders—she's shaping a legacy of empowered, unstoppable women."

—**Shawn P. Neal, Founder and Trusted Leader in Audio Strategy & Production for Communications**

"Business at the core isn't about numbers, products, services, or operational excellence. At the core, it's an embodiment of one person's or team's life giving to another person/group what they need for the next step in their life. No one understands this more than Ally. She understands it's her emotion connecting with your emotion and she's one of the rare humans who can turn emotion into detailed execution and results. When her clients work with her, it is transformative."

—**Jeremy Barr, CEO at Super Founder Global Network**

"Ally possesses a magnetic momentum that's impossible to ignore. It's evident in the way she speaks, the way she moves, and the unwavering belief she has in her message. Her vision has a gravity to it, pulling you towards your most actualized self, like a force of nature.

From the fateful moment I stumbled upon her Instagram Live, my life took an exciting new trajectory. Soon after, I found myself at her San Diego event, Wealthy Woman Live, sharing my own story on her stage and forging connections within her vibrant community. The ripple effect was undeniable—the Wealthy Woman movement has expanded my horizons and my network, leading to collaborations and a deeper immersion in the world of empowered women.

This energy translates into everything Ally does. She masterfully blends chic branding and potent messaging with boss-level confidence and body language that speaks volumes about her authority and expertise.

But beyond her business acumen and magnetic presence, Ally genuinely cares about the women in her movement. Our connection has evolved into a treasured friendship, and future-casting with her has me both excited and inspired by what we will co-create. Ally is a catalyst for transformation, and her impact will be felt for generations to come. The world needs more leaders like Ally, and I'm excited to be a witness to her rising star."

—Alia Chaaraoui, Founder, Aura Merkabah

"I highly suggest working with Ally. She's going to get inside what you're currently doing. Sometimes we just need someone to step back and look at what we're doing and peel back what we need to change and how we need to market it. Something that I highly suggest is especially having one on one [coaching]. A lot of times we get stuck in these group programs, and you don't get the same amount of help that you really need. Because a lot of times, in a group training program, they're not going to look at your offer, and they're not going to look at the inside of your business. So having someone to step inside and just be like, do this, don't do that... it's a big, big help. It will cut down a ton of time and a lot of confusion on your end. So you're not trying to figure everything out on your own. Because when you waste time in a business, you waste money."

—Megan Habina, Founder of Valkyrie Fitness

SPEAK YOUR WAY TO WEALTH

The Wealthy Woman Way to Unlock
Exponential Influence, Impact
Millions Worldwide, and Collapse
Your Monthly Income into a Day

ALLY KENNEDY

© 2024 Ally Kennedy

Wealthy Woman Press
San Diego, California

Editor & Interior Design: Lilly Penhall, Stellar Design

Cover Design: Ally Kennedy

All rights reserved. No part of this book may be reproduced by any mechanical, photographic, or electronic process, or in the form of a phonographic recording; nor may it be stored in a retrieval system, transmitted, or otherwise be copied for public or private use—other than for "fair use" as brief quotations embodied in articles and reviews—without prior written permission of the publisher.

Paperback ISBN: 979-8-9919143-0-7

1st Edition: November 2024

Printed in the United States of America

WEALTHY WOMAN *Society*

My intention is to change your life within the pages of *Speak Your Way to Wealth*.

However, unlocking exponential influence, impacting millions worldwide, and collapsing your monthly income into a day becomes a whole lot easier when you have a proven step-by-step system, community, and personalized mentorship to plug in to daily... And I want to give you that opportunity inside the **Wealthy Woman Society**.

The **Wealthy Woman Society** is a 6 month mastermind for the Iconic woman who wants to take the fast lane to the top of your industry.

You want to speak in a way that has your audience immediately think "I want to work with her..." and learn how to host events that impact thousands more around the globe and collapse your monthly income into a day. But more importantly, you'll become the woman who people love to buy high-ticket offers from.

Inside, we'll focus on scaling your impact, influence, and offers the Wealthy Woman Way, which you'll see broken down step-by-step inside of *Speak Your Way to Wealth*.

We have more client success stories than in the pages of this book. Here are a few of my favorites...

- Doing $100,000 in a single weekend with 12 people at her event
- Making $70,000 in a day
- Getting paid $10,000 to travel and speak on stages
- Collapsing my old yearly income into a month, even a day

If you are serious about blowing up your brand and business, you need to be inside the Wealthy Woman Society. DM me on Instagram @theallykennedy to apply.

I cannot wait to see the impact you create on the other side of this book.

DEDICATION

To my mother, Cathy for teaching me how to lead with love. I wish you could see the impact we're making in the world. You'd be so proud.

To my first speaking mentor, Shawn for believing in me. For putting me In the Arena. For seeing something in me that I didn't yet see in myself.

CONTENTS

Foreword... vii

Introduction
How I Turned a $49 Mic Into
My Old Yearly Salary in 21 Days 1

I: The Wealth Zone
Become a Match for High Paying Clients
and Collapse Time Around Money...................... 13

II: The Wealthy Woman Way
Scale Your Impact, Influence, and
High-Ticket Offers at Lightning Speed.................. 37

III: Six Figure Speaker System
How to Host Events That Impact Millions Worldwide
and Collapse Your Monthly Income into a Day 90

IV: Wealthy Woman Society
Take the Fast Lane to the Top of Your Industry and
Implement Every Strategy in a Single Weekend......... 110

V: Wealthy Speaker Workshop
Shape a Message That's a Match for Millions
to Deliver from Your Own Events, or to Share
from Stages Around the World........................ 146

FOREWORD

Your ability to communicate is not merely a skill; it is a gateway to greatness. If you want to be known around the world, move people, attract wealth, impact lives, and transform your community, the number one skill you must master is the art of SPEAKING.

For many years, I have been fortunate to know Ally Kennedy, a radiant force within the Freedom Queen movement since its inception. Watching her journey as a true leader in the speaking arena has been nothing short of inspiring. Ally has dedicated countless hours, invested thousands of dollars, and poured her heart into mastering the art of speaking—not just to inform, but also to sell, transform, and lead. Her commitment to understanding what resonates with audiences from the stage is unparalleled.

I've seen Ally refine her skills, breaking down the nuances of persuasive communication that elevate a simple presentation into a compelling call to action. After all, simply performing, talking, or creating a PowerPoint won't build a million-dollar company. It's learning "The Wealth Woman Way" that will.

When I was planning my first conference, I immediately knew that Ally was the perfect choice to support my speakers on this vital subject. Truly the only subject that matters in life and business. I recommended her to many of our top speakers, and the feedback I received was extraordinary. They said, "Ally knows exactly what she's talking about," and "She's not just teaching me how to be confident on stage; she's teaching me how to MOVE people." That's exactly what I wanted for my speakers: to transform the lives of those listening.

In *Speak Your Way to Wealth*, Ally unveils her entire event system, guiding you to become a world-class speaker. As you immerse yourself in these pages, be prepared to awaken the speaker within you. The lessons you discover will ripple through every facet of your life—your marketing, your coaching, your relationships, and even the dialogue you have with yourself. Witness as your entire existence transforms.

I invite you to embrace the wisdom woven in every single page of *Speak Your Way to Wealth*, for the world is eagerly awaiting the unique magic of your voice.

Sincerely,
Bridget James Ling
Freedom Queen

INTRODUCTION

HOW I TURNED A $49 MIC INTO MY OLD YEARLY SALARY IN 21 DAYS

"The game is to realize that 'what to do' is important, but surrender to the fact that your energy is more powerful."
—Ally Kennedy

I CAN BARELY GET OUT OF BED.

It's 12pm and I'm staring at the ceiling. I want to close my eyes and go back to sleep. It's been weeks of disappointment. Questioning myself.

I can't get this out of my head… "Ally, you've been scaling brands for a decade… why can't you scale yours?"

I felt defeated. I didn't understand. I hired the best sales and marketing mentors in the world…

I had all of the things I was told I "needed" to sign more clients. The ads, the funnels, the fancy tech. You name it. I was "doing all the things" and experiencing slow growth.

I kept investing into all of these cookie cutter strategies—scripts and frameworks to sell with Facebook groups, how to sell on Instagram stories, how to craft the perfect carousel conversion framework… you name it.

I felt frustrated investing into program after program. Joining every group coaching program, course, and mini-mind I could get my hands on, trying to find the missing strategy.

I felt like I was banging my head against the wall. I was watching everyone else in the industry celebrating their highest months ever…

Thinking "It's MY TURN."

Before I started my coaching business, I was driving the business strategy for a billion dollar brand, TaylorMade Golf. I just doubled their annual revenue in 10 months flat.

I went from the top of one industry… to what felt like the bottom of a new industry.

I was making good money, but based on who I am and what I knew I was capable of… I felt like I should be further along. I was living on sales calls. Sending 100s of DMs. I had zero room for creativity. Business felt heavy.

And I was thinking to myself, "There has to be a better way than this…"

I knew it was meant for massive impact. I wanted to help more people. But I didn't know where to go from here. Have you ever felt deep in your bones that you're meant for so much more? That's where I was… And I was willing to do anything… willing to pay anything to bring my vision to life. I knew I was meant to impact thousands more women around the world… but I didn't know where to go from here.

I remember sitting on the floor at my altar in my office… I asked God for a sign.

"What do I do next?"

I pulled an oracle card, with a photo of the desert that read, "Vision Quest." I opened the book and read…

> A *"vision quest" is a process whereby you spend a few days in the wilderness alone. Many who have completed a vision quest assert that it is a powerful and even life changing experience, and report vivid and profound revelations. The desert is an ideal place to seek a vision or, more accurately, to allow a vision to come to you. It is time for you to go on a vision quest."*

My mind is racing… "Do I go to Joshua Tree? The Dunes?" I open my computer to google the closest desert to San Diego…and staring me right in the face is an email at the top of my inbox.

"LIVE EVENT IN ARIZONA"

The mentors I hired were hosting a mastermind event in Scottsdale, AZ… **in the Desert**. My body immediately told me… "This is the vision quest."

I never whipped out my credit card so fast in my life. Within minutes, I purchased my ticket. Something inside me immediately shifted by saying, "Yes..." The feeling of possibility set my soul on fire, thinking, "what if this event is the thing that changes my life..."

And even though I already decided to go, there was a war waging in my mind. Have you ever felt like you're not far enough along yet? Like you need to hit a certain milestone to feel qualified?

That's where I was. I felt so much resistance about getting in the room with successful entrepreneurs making $50K, $100K, $500K months....I didn't feel like I belonged at that event. I had every excuse not to go.

But I'm so glad I did, because everything changed for me in that room.

Have you ever seen magic happen in a moment?

That's what I felt like I was witnessing as I saw the speakers changing lives right in front of my eyes. Screaming, cheering, moving people to tears... the speakers were creating these amazing experiences using their voice. I wanted to do that.

The next day, there was an award ceremony. I remember watching some of the clients walking on stage to collect their Million Dollar awards, thinking, "What's the difference between them and me?"

Have you ever been in a program with someone... you started at the same time... and one person's business skyrockets... and the other one... well... grows a lot more slowly?

That's where I was. We all had the same scripts. The same curriculum. Access to the same weekly coaching calls. But some of us were making millions... and some were not.

I knew there had to be something more than just what to do... Because I was doing all of it. I was investing tens of thousands of dollars into mentorship. Posting daily, doing weekly livestreams, monthly launches, following my mentor's step-by-step methodology to a T.

I became obsessed with trying to find a pattern... so I spent the rest of the weekend observing the most successful people in the room... and it wasn't long until I found it.

The most successful entrepreneurs in the room had one thing in common...

There was a different energy about them. An energy in how they were leading. An energy in the way they carried themselves. An energy in the way they spoke.

It wasn't just what they were doing... It was who they were being. There was an energy of certainty and conviction with every move they made. With every word they spoke.

And that weekend...

I felt the electricity in that room... and it shifted my identity on a cellular level. There is a level of intensity in your soul that can't be taught... But it can be caught...

And it spreads like wildfire. And after spending 3 days in that room... **that event set my soul on fire.**

Before, I was so in my head about everything. I didn't feel connected to my vision. I was chasing money milestones. I was so attached to the money... looking for it to validate me. I was placing my happiness in how much money I was making... and whether or not I hit my goals that month.

But that room woke something up inside me. It woke up an emotion. It woke up a new identity... I didn't want to let it go.

And you're gonna experience some similar things in this book. And I want you at this moment to make some commitments...

- To speak
- To make more money
- To wake up the world
- To get known around the world for your life-changing work

To commit to whatever it is you want to do. To activate a new level of conviction in yourself, your ability, your story, your process, your method, your mission, your movement...

And feel a moral obligation to share it with the world in a <u>much bigger way.</u>

That's what that event did for me, and that's what I wanna do for you inside of Speak Your Way to Wealth. I know most people read self-help books and don't do anything with them, so they turn into shelf-help books... and they lose all the momentum they create.

But you're not most people.

Even at that event, I remember hearing one of the speakers say...

> "Most people give up. Most people talk a lot but they don't follow through. Even in this room, all of you had a great experience, but only 1% of you will follow through. Only a small handful will take what you learned, apply it, implement it and CHANGE THE WORLD."

When he spoke those words, something landed so profoundly in my body. I didn't start this business to make money on social media. I started my business to change the world.

I left my corporate job driving the business strategy for a billion dollar brand job in 2021, because after my mom passed away, making money for businesses lost all meaning.

At that moment... I realized that I built the job I escaped from... chasing numbers. And I'll never forget that moment because that was the moment I decided I was done chasing money milestones... Instead...

I decided to chase *impact*.

I felt a new level of power rushing through my veins as I decided...

"I'm not meant to sit in this audience. I'm meant to speak on the stage."

In that moment, I declared, **"I AM A SPEAKER."**

A wave of relief rushed through my body. I immediately felt lighter. I shifted from feeling pressure... feeling like I was pushing to hit a goal... to be carried... to being pulled by my vision.

At that event, they made an offer, and it was more than double what I was making per month... but I knew I needed to be in that room. I knew I needed to stay in that energy... so of course I ended up signing up for it.

That event impacted my life so profoundly, I decided I was done just sitting in my office, selling on social media to grow my business.

I bought a $49 mic from Amazon and hosted my first in-person event. I launched my first high-ticket mastermind. I started speaking to sell...

And that $49 mic turned into my old yearly salary in 21 days.

And I remember thinking to myself... **"Why would anyone NOT take this seriously?"**

One event, *when done right*, has the power to change the trajectory of your entire life.

When you see someone like Taylor Swift on stage... she is a billionaire from her events because she mastered the words to the songs. Because she put her personality, her stories, and her magic into her songs. That's why she makes rockstar money.

And speaking? It's kinda the same.

When you master the words to the song, you get the rockstar treatment. You can make six-figures in a single weekend from your event, just like my client Amanda, who I'll tell you more about later.

You can impact millions and make millions as a speaker.

This was the beginning of becoming obsessed with what makes it work. I began hiring... even flying to train in person with the best in the industry.

I infused speaking into my brand, marketing, the way I sell, and coach.

Within two years, I turned my boring coaching business into a global movement. My business skyrocketed, and I was invited by the eight-figure coaches who hosted that Scottsdale event, to share my proven methods (the same ones I am teaching you in this book) from the stage. All expenses paid.

And after speaking at, consulting on, and selling from the stage of events bringing in a total of $5.2 Million in client sales… sharing stages with some of the top names in the coaching industry… **I became known in my industry**.

I became sought after to help clients have six and seven-figure days. Today, I'm regularly hired by seven- and eight-figure entrepreneurs to help them speak from stage, consult on, or sell from their events.

I became known as the best in the industry when it comes to speaking to sell in a way that positions you as a Category of One in your industry and creates an Instant Influence Identity (a.k.a. people find you, trust you immediately and buy from you without months of warming up).

I have collapsed my old yearly salary into my monthly income, normalizing five-figure days, and getting paid up to five-figures to speak on a single stage… while having more space on my calendar and traveling more than ever.

Outside of the impact I make online…I get paid to travel and speak from stages around the world.

On top of that, I'm the official speaker trainer and only one endorsed by top leaders and companies in the industry to train the speakers for their events.

But more than that, I feel so much fulfillment outside of money because I am living a bigger purpose. I have so much conviction in my work because of the impact I'm making with my message.

I feel so powerful being able to deliver my body of work through events that have DMs flooding in for weeks saying,

"Your event changed my life…"
"I'm still having breakthroughs…"
and "How can I hire you?"

It was in a way that attracts the most self-led, empowered clients into our Wealthy Woman Society Mastermind and 1:1 mentorship spaces. When so many people started asking me, "How did you do it?" I knew I needed to create a system.

In the process, the **Wealthy Woman Way** was born.

The **Wealthy Woman Way** was designed to help you to scale your impact, influence and offers as a speaker. It has three pillars…

- Build a High-End Brand with An Instant Influence Identity
- Create Category of One Messaging that Moves the Masses
- Speak to Sell Your High-Ticket Offers

When you nail all three?

You take the fast lane to the top of your industry, speak in a way that has your audience immediately thinking, "I want to work with HER…"

You learn how to host events that impact thousands more around the globe and collapse your monthly income into a day.

But more importantly, you'll BECOME the woman who people LOVE to buy high-ticket offers from.

Your income is a direct reflection of the way you speak to sell.

If you don't know how to articulate the value of your work… you're not going to make it big.

I wrote *Speak Your Way to Wealth* to show you how to impact millions worldwide, and collapse your monthly income into a day with speaking. Because it's my mission to make sure that your sales are not just transactional, they're transformational.

Speak Your Way to Wealth isn't a book to help you make money. It's a road map to unlocking a wealthy life. It disrupts the old, outdated paradigm of "traditional" business... breaking all the rules and flipping it on its head.

And while we'll cover "what to do" to impact and make millions... The game is to realize that "what to do" is important, but surrender to the fact that your energy is more powerful...

And it is the key to you growing your business at lightning speed. *Speak Your Way to Wealth* is only as powerful as you chose to integrate it into your business and the way you lead.

Here is how to experience the biggest transformation from this book:

In **Part One**, you will shift out of your head and into your power. There is a cap to what you can do, but there's no limit to who you can be. You'll learn how to get into The Wealth Zone (and stay there), so you can become the woman who continuously multiplies your income in every season of business. You'll feel unshakable no matter how many sales are coming in, or what number is in your bank account. As a result of exploding your personal power, you'll see a massive shift in your results when implementing the step-by-step strategy in the following chapters.

In **Part Two**, you'll discover the Wealthy Woman Way to scale your impact, influence and offers. You will learn and implement the foundational pieces that you need in your brand, messaging, and sales strategy to become the woman who people LOVE to buy high-ticket offers from. You'll craft messaging that has high-level clients thinking, "you're speak to my soul…" (and pay in full), and discover the #1 wealth building skill in the world. This will turn your current ceiling into your new floor, so you can create true freedom to sell what you want & live how you want.

In **Part Three**, you'll walk step-by-step through the Six Figure Speaker System to launch your next virtual or in-person event. By the end of this section, you'll learn how to speak in a way that has your audience immediately think "I want to work with HER." You'll understand what creates a momentum stronger than a category 5 hurricane that has attendees whipping out their credit cards faster than you can say "Pay in Full" — joining your highest ticket offers within minutes of dropping them from your events. This is how you will collapse your monthly income into a day, impact thousands more around the globe, and turn your body of work into the vehicle for a global movement.

In **Part Four**, you'll learn how you can compress time as you implement everything you learned in this book in a single weekend, so you can go even further, even faster.

By the end of *Speak Your Way to Wealth*, every part of your business will level up, becoming more potent and powerful. You will multiply the effectiveness of every single email, post, and event you create... watching your results compounding faster than ever.

Before you know it, you'll become sought out, hired by clients at your highest price points, and you'll see an extra 0 staring back at you at the end of your bank account. You'll think, "This is what influence feels like—being in demand, being in control, being the woman everyone wants to learn from."

I cannot wait to see the impact you create on the other side of this book.

The most powerful way to experience this book is by reading every single word, moving with lightning speed as you implement the homework sections, and take every opportunity presented to you inside of *Speak Your Way to Wealth*.

It's time to move the masses with your message.

I'll see you inside.

XO
Ally

I: THE WEALTH ZONE

BECOME A MATCH FOR HIGH PAYING CLIENTS AND COLLAPSE TIME AROUND MONEY

"It only takes a moment to decide to step into a new version of yourself."
—Ally Kennedy

"WHY DID YOU HIRE ME?"

I asked my new mastermind clients on the tail end of the launch that brought in my old yearly salary in 21 days.

I was genuinely curious...

Because I was doing "all the things" for about a year and a half... and although I was signing on high-ticket, 1:1 clients...

This was my first "successful" group program launch where I brought in a volume of high-ticket clients in a short period of time.

"I saw you step into your power... and I knew you could help me step into mine."

My mind was blown.

Because after 4 years of coaching and investing over $100,000.00 on mentorship...

I never heard a single mentor teach me this.

They want you to think you need to work harder.

They say...

"Just up your ad spend. Get a good conversion rate. Get more people on the phone. Send more DMs. Hire an appointment setter. Run another masterclass. Create more viral videos."

And right now, you need to get a little mad... because you've been lied to.

You don't need to post 2-3X a day, create the perfect carousel, viral reel, or be on every platform at once...

You don't need to _do_ more.

Unlocking your next level of wealth isn't about working harder, it's about working higher.

Most of these people go through life thinking that they have to _do_ more to be successful. But the truth is, that they have just never learned to deliver value on a higher Level.

The lowest level of value in the marketplace? It's implementation. It's working with your hands. It's _doing_.

And the highest level of value in the marketplace? It's communication. Using your voice to deliver value. *Think: speaking.* And imagination. Dreaming up innovative ways to bring your work to life. Creating new worlds and immersive experiences. *Think: events.*

The highest level of value in the marketplace has little to do with _doing_ and everything to do with _being_.

Why?

Because there is a cap to what you can do. But there is no limit to who you can be.

So before I teach you what to do to scale your impact, influence, and offers as a speaker, we need to have an important conversation so you don't just get some results implementing what you learn inside *Speak Your Way to Wealth*... You get insane results.

Without the principles you'll learn in this chapter, what to do won't land as powerfully.

How do I know?

FOR SO LONG, I WAS ONLY FOCUSED ON "WHAT TO DO" TO HIT MY NEXT MILESTONE.

I was doing all of the things I was told I "needed" to sign more clients...

My income was still plateaued. I felt like I needed to convince people of the value of my work. I was constantly hearing, "I can't afford it," and "You're so inspiring!" and "One day I'll work with you!"

When I sent the link, I was ghosted in the DMs. It took months, even years to build trust with my audience before they would join my high-ticket offers. My income was plateaued, and it was affecting how I was feeling day-to-day in my business.

You know when your happiness depends on whether you hit your next $10K, $20K, or $50k+ month? Or when you're launching a new offer and you feel like you need to get 10 clients to sign on for you to deem it a "successful" launch?

That's where I was. I kept telling myself, "When I have $10K a month, I'll be a "successful" business coach…" And every month that I didn't have a $10K month… I lost a little bit more confidence. And once the first of the month rolled around, I got back on the hamster wheel, running in circles, chasing after that $10K month.

After I shifted from chasing money milestones to getting (and staying) in The Wealth Zone… (which you'll learn more about at the end of this section)

Everything changed.

High-ticket clients started finding and buying from me within minutes. I began getting hired by top leaders in the industry who are "further along" than me, and making more money than me.

Dream clients began enrolling into my highest ticket offers… paying in full from as little as an 8-12 message conversation in the DMs.

It was a complete 180 from the clients I was attracting before. Everyone who reached out for the link was buying.

My income was growing steadily month over month, year over year, without "doing more…" And the clients in my DMs?

They were excited to pay me.

That $10K month? I never hit it. I jumped right to $30K a month. And I'm about to show you exactly how.

NO MATTER WHERE YOUR NEXT INCOME GOAL IS… I'M ABOUT TO SHOW YOU HOW YOU CAN SKIP STEPS ON YOUR WAY THERE.

Because you're meant for something so much more.

More clients. More impact. More visibility. More depth. More transformation. More DMs saying, "You're speaking to my soul… how can I work with you?"

You're done being in rooms that are just talking about how to make $10K, $20K, $50K+ months from social media.

That's your bare minimum.

You want to impact thousands more around the world speaking and hosting events.

You're ready for a space that's normalizing five and six-figures in a single day from events (even if you're not speaking and hosting events yet, you're ready to stretch yourself for the level of impact and income you're meant for.)

And you'll make this your reality even faster when you understand how to get in The Wealth Zone… And stay there.

But before I tell you what The Wealth Zone is… I want to explain why this is *the thing* that will create quantum leaps in your business.

A quantum leap is the explosive jump that a particle of matter undergoes in moving from one place to another… Without apparent effort, without covering all the "bases" before starting and ending points.

To become the woman who leaps in every season of business… there's a couple things you need to understand. Here's the first one…

WHEN YOU MASTER THESE TWO ENERGIES IN BUSINESS, YOU'LL BECOME THE WOMAN WHO MULTIPLIES YOUR INCOME IN EVERY SEASON.

Would you agree that some things take time?

Creating an offer, growing an audience, planning, executing and hosting an event, completing a launch… Things that you need to grow your business will take you time to implement.

Think about this as long-term energy. Business requires long-term energy. Long-term consistency. Long-term commitment.

While everyone else is thinking in days, in weeks, in timelines… **The most successful entrepreneurs are playing in decades.** We're playing a completely different game. We are climbing the mountain with no peak (I'll share more about this when I help you tap into your Limitless Wealth Identity in Part Three of *Speak Your Way to Wealth*).

And yes, we need strategy to materialize every goal or "mile marker" on the mountain. I believe in strategy. And I promise we will dive deep into strategy in Parts Two and Three of *Speak Your Way to Wealth*.

However, this is where most business mentors stop.

So, we both know that certain things take time. Posting on social media, for example. It takes time to write the copy. It takes time to build an audience.

Selling an offer?

It takes time to create the offer, write the marketing copy, launch it, and fulfill the promise to your clients. Some things are going to take time and you need to be patient.

But what if I told you there was a way to collapse time?

Have you ever seen two people implement the same strategy and get two completely different results? Have you ever wondered why that is? This is where short-term energy comes in.

Short-term energy in business is who you're being. It's your identity. It's how you see yourself. It's how you're leading. It's how you're moving. It's the level of power you're operating in on a daily basis.

The reason this is the key to skipping steps?

Because it only takes a moment to decide to step into a new version of yourself.

Short-term energy is what activates the strategy.

When you combine the foundation of consistency in basic things (income producing activities, following the Wealthy Woman Way which you'll learn in Part Two) with getting in, and staying in The Wealth Zone, which I'll show you how to do at the end of Part One…

Results happen at lightning speed.

This is not a how-to strategy. It comes back to your leadership.

The level of power at which you lead is the thing that will compound the results in your business.

The context of this is being able to hold the duality of what to do and who to be… But surrender to the fact that your energy is more powerful than any strategy.

If you want to become the woman who multiplies her income in every season of business… you need to master the long term, predictable energy of what to do… and consistency in your daily actions…

However, your energy is your number one priority. Who you're being while you implement the day-to-day strategy is what will multiply its effectiveness.

When you rise in your personal power, you enter what I call The Wealth Zone.

You want speed to results? You want to be a match for high-paying clients faster? You want people to find you, immediately feel, "I want to hire HER…" Jumping in your DMs asking for the link faster than you can say, "Pay in Full?"

Your number one priority is to get in The Wealth Zone.

Before we talk about The Wealth Zone, I want you to help you understand the energy of Wealth, because this is the number one thing that keeps most people from making more money.

WEALTH IS NOT MONEY

I wasted so much time thinking… "Once I make six-figures, I'll feel successful in my business."

As entrepreneurs, we get wrapped up in chasing money milestones. The duality is… this is exactly why most people don't hit the goals they want. The milestones (while extraordinary) rarely matter.

Because when you get there? It's almost never as good as you thought.

What you're really after?

It's not the money in your bank account. It's the *feeling* the money will give you.

You don't want a multi-million dollar business, you want the *feeling* of security a multi-million dollar business will give you.

If money is the thing that would make everyone happy… why is it that so many millionaires are unhappy and unfulfilled?

It's because wealth and money are two separate things.

Money is a piece of paper. It is a thing. It is the number in your bank account.

Wealth is a *feeling*. Wealth is *feeling* alive and free. Wealth is the *feeling* that comes from waking up to a mountain view every day. Wealth is the *feeling* of the sun shining on your skin while you're rollerblading next to the ocean dancing to your favorite song.

Wealth is the *feeling* of the first sip of coffee in the morning, sitting outside on the porch, watching the birds, watching the pine needles dance in the wind as the cool breeze hits your face. Wealth is the *feeling* when you've got your hair and makeup done, you're wearing your favorite outfit, you look and smell like a goddess.

Wealth *feeling* rock sold in who you are, without needing anyone telling you how good you are. Wealth is a *feeling*. And it *feels* different for everyone.

Wealth is the feeling you are chasing on the other side of your money milestones... not the money milestones themselves.

So often you think, "I'll be happy when I make $50K/months..." or "I'll be happy when I hit my next million..." or "I'll be happy when I [insert the milestone you're chasing]..."

Wealth is not needing anything outside of you to validate your happiness. Wealth is not needing anything outside of you to feel qualified enough. Wealth is not needing anything outside of you to feel like you've "made it."

Wealth is non-circumstantial power.

Right now, if you think, "When I hit the milestone... I'll feel more confident. Then... I'll show up bigger. I'll take up more space online. I'll raise my prices. I'll have more conviction in my offer. I'll sell with more audacity..."

You've got it backwards.

Because the results you want in your business are a byproduct of tapping into the *feeling* of wealth now.

When you *feel* wealthy, you do not need anyone telling you how good you are... you don't need anything outside of you to validate your happiness. When you *feel* wealthy... You're in your power. You show up with more power. More confidence. More conviction. You make bigger moves. You take risks. You follow your intuition.

You have the ability to *feel* wealthy right now without changing your financial situation.

Wealth is an energy.
Wealth is personal power.
Wealth is not chasing a money milestone to feel validated.

Wealth is continuing to raise the bar over and over and go for higher levels of success because you know who you are and you know what you're capable of.

Do you feel the energetic difference here?

You can make a decision to live in alignment with the energy of wealth.

You don't need more money in your bank account. You don't need to be "further along." You don't need more certifications.

You need to DECIDE that you are the one.

You need to DECIDE that you are the one who is wildly in demand. You are the one who gets paid highly. You are the one who attracts the most extraordinary clients and opportunities. That success is inevitable for you.

It only takes a moment to decide to step into a new version of yourself.

And when you do? Your energy and power shifts to become in alignment with this new version of yourself. And energy will multiply the effectiveness of every strategy you implement in your business.

So often we wait until we have money, clients, external validation to feel successful.

Simon Sinek says, "*Too many people confuse being rich or famous with being a leader. Wealth and fame are byproducts, not qualifications to lead.*"

Myron Golden says, "*Lead generation is the opposite of need declaration.*"

I like to say, "*Stop telling your audience what you need and start showing them how you can lead.*"

Your energy and your power?

It overrides every strategy that I will teach you inside of Speak Your Way to Wealth.

The work I am about to teach you in the next chapter will take you so much further, and so much faster than anybody who is just focusing on strategy. There's an energy to it that doesn't make logical sense.

Before I had my first…

- Client
- Five-figure month
- Multiple five-figure launch
- Multiple five-figure day
- Six-Figures in my stripe account
- Dollar of monthly recurring revenue
- Stage to speak on

I didn't have money in the bank… But I decided "**I AM A WEALTHY WOMAN.**"

So I want you to do one thing today… Decide that you are a Wealthy Woman. Because wealth is not a thing that happens later… Wealth happens now. You are it now. You are her now.

You don't need more money in your bank account to feel wealthy.

But right now…

You're giving your power away to the number in your bank account, the number of clients enrolling during your launches, or the time it takes someone to buy after you send the link…

And it's knocking you out of The Wealth Zone.

But what is The Wealth Zone?

I'm going to show you exactly what it is in the next chapter so you can begin to collapse time around money.

HOMEWORK

- Declare that you are a Wealthy Woman. Say outloud to yourself right now, "I AM A WEALTHY WOMAN." Write "I AM A WEALTHY WOMAN" in this book to declare it. Declare it in a post, or on your Instagram stories and tag me on @theallykennedy so I can celebrate you for embodying your next level of wealth, as this is the first step to attracting it faster.
- What brings you the feeling of wealth? How can you bring more of that feeling into your life today?
- If you knew today would be a $100K day, how would you show up? How would you post? What content would you make? What would you sell? What decisions would you make? How do you show up? How do you dress? Do your hair and makeup? How would you post? How would you talk about your offers? What do your boundaries look like? Pricing? What investments are you making? What actions do you take daily? What do your photos look like? What energy do you lead with? What do you do with your day?
- Which of the above actions can you shift into right now to embody your next level of wealth?

THE WEALTH ZONE

"Immediate IG stalk followed by a binge and an, 'I need to get closer' energy."

This was the message I received from a woman who just found me and bought an offer from me within minutes.

> HI beauty! Just purchased your upgrade for replays of Exponential Influence 🙏 I just joined Bridget's Membership and saw your post in the FB group....
> 💜
>
> Immediate IG Stalk followed by a binge and an, "I need to get closer" energy. Bummed I missed it live & voxer but so excited to catch the replays! Is the 15 minute strategy call still part of this?
> 💜

This is a result of being in The Wealth Zone.

When you're *not* in The Wealth Zone, you're chasing money milestones.

When you are in The Wealth Zone, you're in your power, and you become a magnet for money, making more and more of it while doing less.

The work?

Get in The Wealth Zone. Stay in The Wealth Zone. And protect yourself from things that knock you out of The Wealth Zone.

Allow nothing into your life that takes away from your focus on your mission, or knocks you out of The Wealth Zone.

Have you ever wondered, what's the best strategy? How should I launch this offer? What should I post today to make this the best launch ever?

Truth is...

Every strategy works when you are in The Wealth Zone.

So what does it mean to be in The Wealth Zone?

The Wealth Zone is a frequency. It's an energetic state. It's when you're operating with non-circumstantial leadership and non-circumstantial power. You're so tapped into your mission, your vision, the value of your work. You're pioneering, you're trailblazing, you're innovating. You're in flow.

When you are in The Wealth Zone, you're focused on service, delivering your work, moving the masses with your message, and delivering insane value.

Getting in The Wealth Zone is kinda like choosing to walk through a door that is open to you right now, no matter what your external circumstances look like.

When you walk through that door, it's kinda like you enter a vortex of energy that pulses through every vein, and shoots up, out of your head like an antenna, sending magnetic waves out that attract the most extraordinary clients and opportunities.

When you're in The Wealth Zone, you feel like your soul is on fire. You're performing at your highest level. People find you & immediately feel "I need to be in her world…"

When you're not in The Wealth Zone, you need the income and the outcome to validate you… When the reality is, your results are a reflection of your ability to get in The Wealth Zone and stay in The Wealth Zone.

So what does it like when you're in The Wealth Zone vs. Chasing Money Milestones?

When you're in the Wealth Zone...	When you're chasing Money Milestones...
You think... "This offer is so good, it's going to transform so many lives. This offer is important to me, so how am I going to launch it so people go crazy? What's the energy behind it? What does the branding look like? How do I make this the best launch ever?"	You think, "How do I get people to see the value in this offer?" You wonder, "Is this gonna work?"
You're connected to the value of your offer, the vision for the branding, experience of the launch. You think, "This is a masterpiece. How can I blow everyone's mind with this offer?" How can I present this offer to the world in a way that's never been done before?"	You're overthinking, "What if they don't like it? What if they don't buy it?"
You love the journey, you love the process. What other people are doing, how much money other people are making, how many people are watching and not moving, how much money you made last month, or where you're at this month doesn't matter.	You're comparing yourself to other leaders. You're focused on how much money others are making, and how much money you're not yet making. You think, "They're more successful than me... maybe I should do what they're doing..."
You're so in flow, you lose track of time. Time doesn't phase you, because you're in your power, and you know it's your power that creates results, not time.	You're stuck in scarcity, so you feel constricted by time. You look at the calendar and think, "There's only one week left in the month left to hit my goals..." or "There's only two days left in this launch to hit my launch goal..."

When you're in the Wealth Zone...	When you're chasing Money Milestones...
You know that people respond to you... so you ask yourself, "Who do I need to be today to blow it out of the water?" Or "Who do I need to be to double my income?"	You think more money is a byproduct of doing more. You think, "What do I need to do today to get more people to buy?"
You're bold. You're direct. You write content that sounds exactly like you're talking to your girlfriend at dinner after two glasses of wine. You know your authentic expression has to shine to impact the most people.	Creating content feels like pressure. It feels like you need to pull the words out of you. You stare at a blinking cursor on the screen thinking, "What do I say so people buy?"

When you're chasing Money Milestones... you're focused on what to do to get your next clients.

You're in a grippy, needy energy, looking for clients. Sales feel heavy.

When you are in The Wealth Zone... you're focused on who to be to become a match for your next level of leadership and impact... You're in your own lane. There is a magnetism in your leadership, in your power, that people feel. As a byproduct... clients are looking for you.

They think, "What is going on over there? I want to be in your world." You open your inbox to DMs from the most empowered, self led clients saying, "How can I work with you?" Sales feel as easy as breathing.

Dream clients feel your energy. They flock to you. They buy from you.

The work?

Get in The Wealth Zone.
Stay in The Wealth Zone.
Protect The Wealth Zone.

Don't say, "I'm not in The Wealth Zone today so I won't make money." Consciously decide to get in The Wealth Zone. Value yourself enough to make being in The Wealth Zone and staying in The Wealth Zone a priority.

If something knocks you out of The Wealth Zone?

Put a boundary on it. Remove it from your life. Or decide that it cannot knock you out of The Wealth Zone.

Being in The Wealth Zone is your #1 money maker.

Set your life and business up so nothing knocks you out of The Wealth Zone.

And when you fall out of The Wealth Zone… because you're human and you will…

Get back into The Wealth Zone as quickly as possible.

This is about having compassion. This is about consciously deciding that your past results do not determine your current reality (I'll talk more about this in Part III when I show you how to collapse your monthly income into a day).

Getting into The Wealth Zone and staying there takes a commitment to leading yourself in a way that most are unwilling to.

Getting into The Wealth Zone and staying there is kinda this style of climbing I use while I'm training to climb Tahquitz, a 8,846' mountain. It's called traditional climbing (aka "trad").

Which basically means there are no preset bolts in the wall to clip your draws and rope into… so you create your own route on the wall by placing protection (aka spring loaded cams you jam into cracks) instead of clipping into bolts in a preset route.

You're basically dangling from the side of the mountain on a few pieces of spring loaded metal bits. The thing about climbing trad is that it's technical. It's also scary AF.

There's a lot of nuances in placing the gear and building the anchor. If you place the gear correctly, it won't come out... And you keep climbing, higher and higher up the mountain.

If you don't place the gear correctly... it will come out, and you'll take a big fall.

But there's something about doing big things like trad climbing that sets my soul on fire...

It leads me to my edge. It shows me what I'm capable of holding, mentally and physically... and who I become in the process blows my mind. So dangle it is.

Trad climbing is kinda like getting in The Wealth Zone and staying there.

You're blazing your own trail.

Getting in The Wealth Zone is and staying there isn't always the easiest thing to do when you're climbing to new peaks in your business, just like when you're climbing a mountain.

It takes practice. It takes resilience. It takes a willingness to go places that scare you. It takes facing your fear, and moving anyway...

It takes a willingness to lead at your edge, making big moves that scare you. It takes trusting that if you fall, you're safe. You just need to get back on the wall and keep climbing.

Getting in The Wealth Zone and staying there while you're climbing to your next peak in business is kinda like climbing an 8,846' mountain.

You want to lock arms with someone who's been to the peak you're climbing.

You want a partner that knows the route. You want a partner that can hold the rope when you fall, and knows how to keep you in The Wealth Zone on the way to the top.

Embodying new levels of leadership and power, so that you can stay in The Wealth Zone, is kinda like rock climbing because it isn't something you learn in a book, in a digital course, on a zoom call.

The fastest way is by getting on the wall and climbing. Getting in The Wealth Zone and staying there is the same.

The fastest way to get in The Wealth Zone and stay there is to get In the Arena as a speaker.

But what does that mean?

Let's break it down.

THE FASTEST WAY TO GET INTO THE WEALTH ZONE IS THE SAME THING THAT TOOK LILLY FROM SELLING A $222 OFFER TO A $25,000 OFFER...

"Kinda like… a room full of badass women who just wanted to build shit."

Lilly said, painting the vision of a female mastermind community.

At the time, we didn't know many high-performing entrepreneur women. We met in a sales and marketing coaching program. When I realized we both lived in San Diego, I asked her if she wanted to meet up and do a photoshoot for each other's brands. The rest was history. We started to regularly meet to co-work on our businesses.

"I wish there was an entrepreneur community in San Diego with more powerhouse women who wanted to mastermind and build their businesses…" she said.

In that moment… I felt like time slowed down. I looked up from my laptop. I felt my eyes widen.

"Let's build it."

I never felt so much conviction behind a new idea in my business.

I just got back from the Scottsdale event that changed my life. And for the few weeks after, I looked everywhere online trying to find an event with a similar energy. I went to meetups, women's circles and joined dozens of Facebook groups.

I found lots of events with women journaling about the businesses they wanted, but none of them where women were showing up boldly, taking massive action to make that a reality…

So I decided to build it myself.

"When should we host the event?" I asked.

Within minutes we picked a date. Within days I made a post to gauge interest. Within 48 hours, there were over 200 comments from women who wanted in. Within the week we were selling tickets.

Within six weeks we were in the room facilitating an experience in a room full of women who never commented on a single post of mine, but purchased tickets and drove hours to get in the room with us.

I'll never forget who I became because of that event. I remember crying tears of gratitude in the yin yoga parking lot. I never wanted to forget that movement. I pulled out my video camera and started recording…

"I'm so in love with who you are and who you're becoming. I'm so proud of you… mom would be so proud of you."

On the backend of that event, I launched a mastermind that brought in $31K in 21 days. It took me a year to make that as a hairstylist. Women said they were hiring me because they saw me step into my power.

Within weeks, I got invited to fly to Orlando to speak on my first stage in front of 500 entrepreneurs. Within weeks I received my first all expense paid speaking opportunity.

What I realized?

This wasn't an event. It was a portal to embody new levels of power and leadership.

The women who left that room were starting new businesses, raising the prices, signing on high-ticket clients, and having their highest cash months in business. The testimonials coming in were insane.

That event changed the lives and businesses of every woman who attended... So naturally, I said, "Let's do it again..." Running the event in person, then virtually, then in person, then virtually.

Every time we ran an event, we were receiving messages saying, "your event changed my life..." However, I noticed even bigger shifts from the women who were speaking on the stage.

This was when I decided to start putting our mastermind clients In the Arena.

"I have 100x more confidence in my ability to speak publicly about my program and I feel like an expert in a lot of areas because of that. The workshop I did helped people and I got amazing feedback from everyone about my speaking and my program."

This was a response from Lilly after we put her In the Arena to speak on stage at Wealthy Woman Live. She came out of that event a different woman. Speaking unlocked a new level of power and leadership in Lilly... catapulting her into The Wealth Zone.

She channeled that energy into a new program, immediately launched it. She was convicted in her work. She knew the value in her offer. She saw herself as the one to hire first. As a result? So did her audience. When she dropped her offer? Clients immediately responded, whipping out their credit cards. She signed on 5 clients within the next few days.

From there, she recognized a higher level of value in her work, and decided to go even bigger. She decided what she wanted to be paid, and crafted a new $25,000 offer for her highest level, dream clients... a white glove, premium, done-for-you experience.

Cool part?

That offer is how we wrote this book in a single weekend.

Today? Lilly's getting so many word of mouth referrals for her done-for-you publishing offers that she doesn't need to promote her publishing offers on the front end.

Why does this matter?

Because getting In the Arena as a speaker unlocked a new level of power and certainty in Lilly. She moved with that energy, creating her highest level, dream offer, for her dream client, lifting her price to match the level at which she valued her work.

Your price is a reflection of your certainty. Sales is a transfer of certainty. And when you're in The Wealth Zone, you're connected to the value of your work, so you have the certainty price what you want to be paid, not what you hope people will pay. When you're in the Wealth Zone, you're a match for high-ticket, high-paying clients who don't bat an eyelash at even your highest prices.

You make the most money when you're in The Wealth Zone... and speaking is the ultimate way to unlock new levels of certainty, conviction, and personal power that propel you into The Wealth Zone.

Now that you know that getting in the Wealth Zone and staying in the Wealth Zone is how you make the most money, and what activates the strategy...

In the next chapter, I'm going to walk you through the Wealthy Woman Way, and show you the exact step-by-step strategy to unlock Exponential Influence, impact millions worldwide, and collapse your monthly income into a day with speaking.

HOMEWORK

- Are you running your business from the energy of needing an outcome to validate you? Or are you running your business in The Wealth Zone thinking, "I am a Category of One."
- What activities get you into The Wealth Zone? How can you do more of them?
- What standards do you need to raise in your life and business to get in The Wealth Zone? What boundaries do you need in place to stay in The Wealth Zone?
- Are your current clients good for you being in The Wealth Zone? Are your current relationships good for you being in The Wealth Zone? Are the people you're following on social media good for you being in The Wealth Zone? If not, what do you need to clean up?
- Who knocks you out of The Wealth Zone? What negative habits do you get to let go of that knock you out of The Wealth Zone?
- What rooms can you get in that will help you get into The Wealth Zone and stay there? Do you have mentorship that activates you and keeps you inside of The Wealth Zone? If not, what rooms are you committing to getting in?

II: THE WEALTHY WOMAN WAY

SCALE YOUR IMPACT, INFLUENCE, AND HIGH-TICKET OFFERS AT LIGHTNING SPEED

"You're speaking to your audience before you ever open your mouth."
—Ally Kennedy

BEFORE I CREATED THE WEALTHY WOMAN WAY…

I was investing money on paid ads, sending 100s of DMs, living on sales calls… I had all of the things I was told I "needed" to sign more clients… and my income was still plateaued.

This led me to questioning everything and eventually turning the entire model upside down.

I decided to break the rules, find a more aligned business model, and free myself from the old, outdated, bro-marketer way of signing clients.

After four solid years of testing everything—investing nearly $100,000 in mentorship… I finally cracked the code, and simplified my business to focus on three main pillars.

The result?

I collapsed my old yearly salary into my monthly income, normalizing five-figure days and getting paid up to five-figures to speak on a single stage… while having more space on my calendar and traveling more than ever.

Outside of the impact I make online… I get paid to travel and speak from stages around the world. On top of that, I'm the official speaker trainer and only one endorsed by top leaders and companies in the industry to train the speakers for their events.

But more than that, I feel so much fulfillment outside of money because I am living a bigger purpose. I have so much conviction in my work because of the impact I'm making with my message.

I feel so powerful being able to deliver my body of work through events that have DMs flooding in for weeks saying:

"I'm STILL having breakthroughs…"
"The way you present it is really impactful…"

"I just listened to it for the third time…"
And, "How can I work with you?"

And sure… The money is amazing, but do you know what's even better?

Being a Wealthy Woman, where you're able to…

- Confidently hold your energy and power between sales, clients, and milestones…
- Keep showing up, no matter what, even when it feels like it's "not working…"
- Hold yourself to a high standard and continue to raise the bar… because no matter what level you're on, you know you're made for so much more.

This combination of energetics and strategy are what separate the ones who make some money… and the ones who make insane money, and take the fast lane straight to the top. Penthouse views of the industry. No lease, no rent. You own the damn building.

You'll quickly notice that the way I teach these concepts is unlike anything you've ever heard before. You won't find this information taught anywhere else. You have used pieces of this puzzle, but you're using them in an ineffective way.

What I'm going to show you over the next few chapters of this book are methodologies that will drastically change the amount of income you bring in every single month, the level of influence you have in your industry, and the number of people you're impacting with your work.

So lean in, and do not skip a single word, as I break down the Wealthy Woman Way for you step-by-step, and give you the keys to your very own Penthouse suite.

Here's how it works…

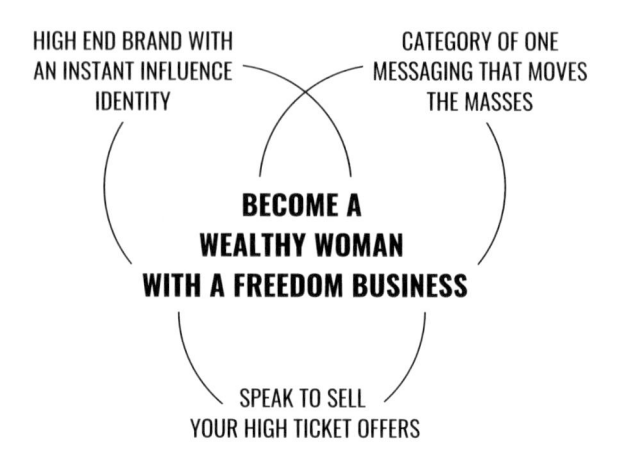

THE **WEALTHY WOMAN** WAY

HIGH END BRAND WITH AN INSTANT INFLUENCE IDENTITY

CATEGORY OF ONE MESSAGING THAT MOVES THE MASSES

BECOME A WEALTHY WOMAN WITH A FREEDOM BUSINESS

SPEAK TO SELL YOUR HIGH TICKET OFFERS

HERE'S WHAT THIS MEANS FOR YOU AND YOUR BRAND…

If you want clients to rush to buy from you on the spot. No sales calls, 100s of DMs, or long landing pages required… To know competition doesn't exist in your industry, because you've created your own industry…

Even your biggest names in your industry thinking, "I need to sign up for her programs…" and reading DMs saying, "Do you have 1:1 availability?"

This is the version of you we'll unleash by scaling your impact, influence, and offers the Wealthy Woman Way.

You'll upgrade your strategy so…

- You 2-3X your rates and see the most empowered clients signing up for your offers
- You know exactly how to speak to attract high-level clients who pay in full

- Every offer you drop sells, no matter the price point or the proximity
- You run events that people remember as "the day that changed everything" and fill your $2,000-$20,000 offers on the spot

You'll upgrade your Instant Influence Identity so...

- Dream clients find you and instantly see *you* as the mentor for them (and buy without months of warming up)
- You feel unshakable in your power. Nothing can knock you out of it, not your income, not people who are watching and not buying
- You raise the bar over and over. Partnering with & speaking on the same stages as Industry Icons you once hired is your new normal
- You impact thousands more around the world & your income will multiply to where it is meant to be

Your current brand, messaging, and price points got you to where you are now, but you know you need to raise the bar for where you're going next...

So let's dive into the first pillar of The Wealthy Woman Way.

BUILD A HIGH END BRAND WITH AN INSTANT INFLUENCE IDENTITY

HOW TO CRAFT A BRAND THAT HAS DREAM CLIENTS THINKING, "I DON'T CARE HOW MUCH IT'S GOING TO COST. I'M GOING TO HIRE HER."

"Not the vibe…"

I thought to myself as I clicked through the websites of videographers.

My biggest speaking gig was coming up, and I was prepared to invest thousands into a videographer to film me facilitating the top event in the coaching industry, guiding the transformation for 400 badass female entrepreneurs.

I was scrolling through hundreds of profiles on Upwork. As soon as I looked at a landing page, I'd instantly think, "Nope…" And scroll by to the next option. Weeks went by… the event was approaching fast. I started to feel anxious because I couldn't find a videographer who met the standards of my brand… but more importantly, someone I felt was a good fit to shadow me for four days I EmCeed the event.

This was a luxury brand, hosting a luxury event. And 99% of the brands I landed on did not say "luxury." They said, "Newbie." They said, "Too masculine." At first glance, my mind instantly said, "I refuse to be seen with this person."

Finally, I caught a lead. I got him on the phone as soon as possible. The moment he opened his mouth to speak? I knew he wasn't for me. His voice was shaky. He spoke slowly. He sounded uncertain. "Nope," I thought… and hung up the phone.

Just as I was about to surrender to the fact that I may not find a videographer in time… I landed on her profile. "Fodor Fotos," it read, next to a picture of a beautiful woman.

To be honest, I almost didn't click on her business name, because she spelled "Photos" with an F, and I didn't trust the spelling of the name. But after I exhausted all of my other options… I went back to her listing. I opened her website… and it was love at first sight.

I was drawn in by the hero image on her website. It was shot beautifully. Cinematic scenes, engaging cuts of video. I was watching the visual story unfold. I immediately thought, "I need to work with HER…."

The black background on her site, clean typography, high contrast, and movie-quality videos screamed "high end" through the screen. I thought, "I'm so glad I found you…" as I submitted an inquiry for the job. Relief flooded my body. And I felt my heart beating faster with excitement… "She's the one. I don't care how much it's going to cost. I'm going to hire her." I thought.

Within the next 24 hours I paid the 50% deposit for her to shoot the 4-day event at a rate of $1,200 per day. On the call, I told her, "Thank God I found you. I am so grateful for you." I was never so excited to send someone money.

Why do I tell you this story?

Because your dream clients are looking for you right now. And the reason 10X more of them aren't reaching out, is because your brand is either attracting or repelling them… before they read a single piece of content, and before they ever get to see your offer.

It takes about 50 milliseconds for someone to form an opinion about your brand that determines whether they'll ultimately stay or leave. I call this the 50 millisecond sale, because you have 50 milliseconds to win the first sale in business… for someone to pay attention.

In order for your dream clients to pay you money, they need to pay attention to you. This is why attention is your most valuable currency as an entrepreneur and marketer of your services. Creating an Instant Influence Identity is the key to getting the *right* attention from your brand.

You don't have an Instant Influence Identity when…

- You're doing "all the things"—sales, marketing, money mindset, posting and selling consistently. Your audience

is growing daily. But based on who you are and the results you're capable of... you know that way more people should be in your $2,000-$20,000 offers.
- You're attracting clients you've outgrown when you know you're ready to be working with a higher-level client.
- You have some clients in your high-ticket offers, but based on how many people buy your low- and mid-ticket offers, you know there should be way more. You get some, "Yes, I'll pay in full!" DMs... but you're still hearing "I can't afford it..." or "Not right now..." when you drop the price of your offers.

Your next level of income and impact it on the other side of elevating every piece of your brand and messaging to become a match for the premium prices you want to be paid.

In this chapter, I'm going to show you exactly what steps to take to shift the energy around your high-ticket offers from, "This is good, but it's not my priority right now..." to "I *need* this..."

MAKING MONEY FEELS EFFORTLESS WHEN...

When you have a High End Brand with an Instant influence Identity... You have an idea, throw out a link, BOOM, a dozen *brand new* people in your audience are joining your world. There's a sense of flow and ease in your business. People find you and are an instant "YES!"

They join at every price without months of warming up. Three-mile long landing pages are not necessary. The energy of being in demand pulses through your veins... igniting you with a deep, embodied confidence—you are no longer chasing opportunities; they are chasing you.

You're seen as the one people love to pay attention to and love to pay. Every offer you drop sells. You wake up to two or three DMs daily from dream clients... from "I'm in..." to "Send me the link..." to "Do you think your $20K package is for me?"

Sales feel easier because you are a living, breathing embodiment of your work. Every piece of content, every program feels like you're creating a masterpiece. You feel so much pride and fulfillment of knowing you've built a movement that's impacting thousands, even millions, of lives. You're having the time of your life and it's magnetic. Your dream clients flock to be a part of everything you create.

When you have a High End Brand with an Instant influence Identity, you are seen as the non-negotiable choice. The <u>only option</u> in your industry.

HOW TO BECOME AN INSTANT "YES" TO HIGH-TICKET CLIENTS

"What you do speaks so loudly that I cannot hear what you say." The first time I heard this quote from Ralph Waldo Emerson it really landed for me.

I like to say, **"You're speaking to your audience before you ever open your mouth."**

Right now, you have a brand, whether you're intentional about it or not. Your brand is how people perceive you. It's how you make them feel. And right now, there are three non-verbal ways you're communicating to your audience through your brand alone.

If you want to get paid high-ticket prices, you need a high-end brand. And If you want clients to be an instant "YES" on you, you need to visually communicate the high quality of your brand.

When it comes to selling high ticket, the look and feel of your brand has the power to influence buying decisions. The first impression of your brand has the power to make someone feel, "I need to work with HER…" Or completely devalue your offer in the mind of your dream client.

Even if you're making good money, when you craft a high-end brand with an Instant Influence Identity — you will multiply your income.

If you think, "I'll work on my brand later" — or if you just don't think it's "that important," remember this...

- If you want more visibility, it's your brand that gets you noticed.
- If you want to eliminate competition, it's your brand that helps you stand out.
- If you want dream clients to see how extraordinary you are, it's your brand that shows them.

So how do you create a High-End Brand with an Instant Influence Identity? I'm going to explain this in a way that no one else teaches. Let's break it down...

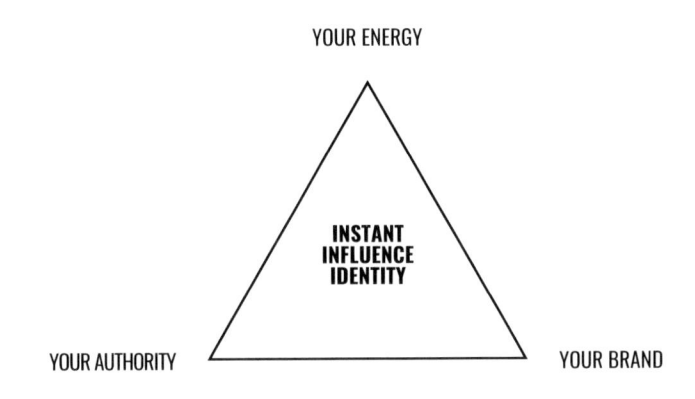

```
              YOUR ENERGY
                  /\
                 /  \
                / INSTANT \
               / INFLUENCE \
              /  IDENTITY   \
             /_____\
        YOUR AUTHORITY      YOUR BRAND
```

PEOPLE MEET YOUR ENERGY BEFORE THEY MEET YOU

People meet your energy before they meet you. Creating an Instant Influence Identity is like embodying the energy of a Diamond in your brand. Diamonds don't question their value.

You don't need to hit the next big milestone, be "further along," or have any "extra evidence" to be an immediate "YES" to high-ticket clients. You need more certainty.

Right now, you're either operating in the energy of YES or NO right now, and your current income is a direct byproduct of it.

Here's how to tell if you're in the energy of YES or NO...

The Energy of Yes...	The Energy of No...
Of course they will buy, because this is the best offer on the internet streets.	Questioning, "Will they buy?"
How is this offer changing the world? How can I articulate that more clearly?	Thinking, "What do I need to say today to create a sale?"
Holding the energy in between every client inquiry, sale, and milestone because you don't need the numbers to validate you.	Dropping an offer & panicking the minute no one buys because you need evidence that it's "working."
Celebrating every DM conversation, application, and sale that comes into your world, no matter the price.	Not feeling grateful or celebratory for every YES, but instead focused on the people who did not say yes
Believing that people love to buy, knowing your work is incredible, and standing behind the value of your work, no matter what.	Only expecting a yes if you discount your offers, stuff it like a turkey full of bonuses, or create massive hype, urgency, and scarcity when promoting your work

When you're the energy of NO, you're in lack. Lack repels abundance. Lack is not a match for being an instant YES. When you're in the energy of YES, you're in the energy of certainty. Sales is a transfer of certainty. The person with the most certainty wins.

Your current level of certainty got you this far... But you know there's another level. You're afraid to claim how good you are at what you do because you don't want to be seen as having a "big ego." You're afraid to speak directly to the results you're capable of getting your best clients because you don't want to be seen as "unethical." You secretly wish someone else would just tell you you're the best instead of you having to claim it publicly...

And that's why there are people who are 10x more successful than you, delivering half the quality you do. It's not because they're "better" than you. They're just more certain than you.

True certainty isn't waiting until you hit your next milestone. Certainty non circumstantial. Certainty is an internal game. Certainty cannot be faked. Certainty creates trust 10X faster, and will collapse time between people finding you and and being an instant "YES" on you.

The high-level, high-paying clients you want?

They will choose certainty over talent every time. They will choose certainty over likeability every time. When it comes to attracting high-ticket buyers who are an instant "YES" on you, their desire (which I'll show you how to create using the Category of One Messaging Method) and your certainty that you can help them achieve that desire are the biggest decision makers.

Your energy speaks louder than your words.

When you embody the certainty of a diamond, you don't need to prove your value. You feel unshakable no matter how many sales are coming in or what number is in your bank account. You simply are. And as a result, clients feel your certainty, and are magnetized to you. This internal confidence builds trust faster, collapses the time between discovery and decision, and turns potential clients into an instant "YES."

Now, let's talk about how this energetic shift plays out into your visuals and messaging to amplify your Instant Influence Identity.

BECOME THE DIAMOND OF YOUR INDUSTRY

Your brand is more than just aesthetics—it's an experience, a feeling, it's how people perceive you. You have a brand whether you're intentional about it or not, because it's the first impression your audience has of you and your work.

Your brand is your differentiation factor. Think about a diamond vs a cubic zirconia. They're both "solutions" to promising a lifelong journey of love & commitment. One is rare & has a higher value. The other is essentially a knock off... an imitation. **Originality, rarity, and uniqueness will always carry more value.** Knock-offs and already-been-done-befores will never compete.

When it comes to your brand, this is about giving yourself permission to innovate. This is about giving yourself permission to approach the way you present yourself, your offers, and your launches with a unique lens and fresh ideas. This is how you position yourself not as just another option, but as the only option.

Your brand should give your audience a taste of what it's like to work with you. Think of it as creating an "emotional preview" through high-quality visuals, storytelling, and design. When you're intentional about every detail, your audience can feel the value you bring before they even step into your programs. They'll recognize the originality, the care, and the power in your brand—and they'll instantly want to be part of it.

Diamonds are prized because no two are exactly alike, and the same goes for your brand. Your Instant Influence Identity isn't just about looking premium—it's about being unforgettable and irreplaceable. This requires recognizing that you are the only one in the world who can do what you do the way you do it. There is no one with your wisdom, your story, your magic. When you see yourself as a premium, one-of-a-kind leader, your brand will reflect that.

In most cases, you're too close to your brand to see your X-Factor, aka the thing that makes you the diamond of your industry. In our highest-level masterminds and mentorship programs, I pull your X-Factor out of you, and work as your creative director alongside our production team to bring it to life visually in a single weekend. The result? A brand that demands attention, and makes your clients immediately feel, "I need to work with *her*."

Now let's talk about the final ingredient for creating an instant "YES…"

WHAT CREATES "I HAVE TO WORK WITH HER," BRAND AUTHORITY…

A diamond doesn't need to shout about why it is the one—it simply shines. Claiming and owning who you are, what you've done, and where you're going is how to shine in your authority.

Claiming your authority doesn't have to be loud or obnoxious, it's about being grounded in your power.

The problem most people run into?

You're afraid to claim your current result because you have shame around your current income level. You're afraid to claim your next level of authority because you're afraid it's going to make you unrelatable. You think, "What if they don't get it?" or "What if they think I'm just in it for the money?" So you water yourself down.

You're not claiming your authority when you're not boldly claiming that you are the one to hire in your marketing, downplaying your success, not sharing client results, lowering your prices out of fear they won't buy, or questioning if your offers are "good enough…"

And the truth is, no one wants to hire a coach who's relatable. Your dream clients pay big to be activated and to be expanded. This is about owning who you are, the results you've created, and showing your audience what's possible for them. If you're too afraid to claim something, you're watering yourself down. And your current level of income is reflecting that.

This is about turning social media into your stage, claiming the spotlight, and shining so bright your audience needs sunglasses.

Quality content, who you're seen with, sharing results, social proof, showcasing what makes your process of getting results unique compared to other solutions in your industry (which you'll learn in the next chapter), and being seen as a speaker will all help you shine brighter in your authority.

"IT'S FUNNY I JUST MET YOU TODAY AND NOW I'M A CLIENT…"

> it's funny i just met you today & now i'm a client 😣 that's how i roll - if it makes sense i make it happen ✌️ 🥂
> 🖤

I opened my DMs to a woman who just joined the Wealthy Woman Society. It read…

And the truth is, you're only a few tweaks this being your reality, too. This is what happens on the other side of building a high-end brand with an Instant Influence Identity.

Creating an Instant Influence Identity is a portal to entering a to your biggest season in business.

It's an invitation to become the woman who sets the standard… who continues to raise the bar… the woman who everyone looks to as an ICON… And your next level of impact and income is born at lightning speed as a byproduct.

A high-end brand with an Instant Influence Identity is the difference between staying where you are and skyrocketing to where you know you belong. A high-end brand with an Instant Influence Identity is the key to waking up to two to three DMs a day from dream clients inquiring about your highest ticket offers, eager to pay any price to work with you, because you're a living, breathing, embodiment of your work.

When you have a high-end brand with an Instant Influence Identity, you're a walking masterpiece. Everything you touch turns to gold. You think… "This is exactly what I imagined… being THE go-to authority in my industry—and now it's my reality…"

You feel unstoppable. You're on fire in every season of business. You move bigger, you take up more space, your content is BOLD, intentional, and powerful… because you know your worth.

When you become a woman with an Instant Influence Identity… This is bigger than a high-end brand… This is legacy leadership.

HOMEWORK

- Picture yourself about to invest $20,000 to hire a new mentor. What draws you to her? What is her brand aesthetic? How does her video presence, confidence, and overall energy make her an instant YES? What about her brand makes you feel, "I need to work with her!" Reflect on these qualities. Where can you apply them to your brand?
- At first glance, would you confidently invest $20,000 in yourself? Take an objective look at your own brand. What needs refining in your presence or messaging to make you an instant "YES"? Identify one thing to clean up or elevate to better match the standards of your dream client.
- Audit your energy. Are you a YES or NO? Examine your videos, body language, posture, and presence. Is every detail giving "YES" energy? Do your call-to-actions and energy exude certainty and confidence, or is there hesitation? Notice where you can step up your presence to radiate more certainty.
- Position your brand as the diamond. Look at your brand through the lens of rarity, originality, and high-end appeal.

Is it clear, intentional, and consistent? If you already ran a multi-seven- or eight-figure brand, what would that look like? How can you start applying that vision today to elevate your brand identity? Add one element this week that reinforces your brand's premium feel and diamond identity in the marketplace.
- Audit your authority. Are you claiming your space as "THE ONE"? Are you showing up with unwavering conviction in your value? Anchor yourself in your results, and don't play small. Decide to step fully into your next level of communicating that you are the obvious choice in your industry. Review your recent posts and videos. Identify one area to refine—whether it's clearer messaging, sharing more client wins, or a more audacious call-to-action—to make your authority unmistakable.

CREATE CATEGORY OF ONE MESSAGING THAT MOVES THE MASSES

"I WANT TO WORK WITH YOU. WHAT'S THE BEST WAY TO DO THAT?"

I posted a carousel on Instagram before I went to bed, and this message was staring me in the face when I opened the app the next morning. It was a DM from a dream client wanting to hire me to help her write her talk for an upcoming event.

Within the next few hours, she paid in full for my In the Arena 1:1 Speaker Training Experience. I continued on with my normal routine. Before I knew it, another DM rolled in…

"You're speaking to my soul. How can I hire you?"

Another client interested in my In the Arena 1:1 Speaker Training Experience. We exchanged a few DMs. Within a few hours she paid in full for the same high-ticket offer. Within the next few weeks, I brought in a total of $22,000 cash from the same offer, from content alone.

No big launch. No free masterclasses. No sales calls.

Every single client messaged me… and in less than 12 DMs they were enrolled into my high-ticket 1:1 offer. This is the result of creating Category of One Messaging that Moves the Masses.

If you don't know how to articulate the value of your work and speak about your offers in a way that has clients thinking, "You're speaking to my soul…"

If you don't have clients lining up to join your high-ticket programs without needing to send 100 DMs or get on a sales call… You need my eyes on your messaging. Right now, you are so close to your own genius that you don't know what the thing is that makes you a Category of One.

There are nuances in your messaging that are still speaking to people who need saving instead of speaking to people who want to go from good to great, or great to extraordinary. This is why you have some of your dream clients inside your comments, DMs, and paid programs… but not 10X more of them.

If you want to know who you're speaking to, look at your comments, DMs, and the clients joining your paid spaces.

Here's how to know it's time to elevate your messaging…

- You have clients joining your spaces who are draining your energy. You feel like you have to hand-hold them. They're not getting extraordinary results and it's causing you to question if your programs are really that good (when they are thebomb.com… you're just speaking to the wrong person in your messaging).
- You're getting some pay in fulls… but you're still hearing, "I can't afford it," when potential clients ask for the link, they don't follow through and buy. When you drop the price of your offer, you get ghosted in the DMs.
- You're describing your work with generic terms like "manifestation," "embodiment," "mindset," and "content…" you're being too macro and blending in with the noise. Your dream client? She can't hear you. Because you're not talking about your micro genius. A.K.A. the things that make you a Category of One… And separate you from thousands of other health, fitness, mindset, business, embodiment, or [insert what you teach] coaches.

Nine times out of ten, when clients come into my world they are too close to their own messaging to see these gaps. And that's why you're making good money… But you're not making insane money. The thing about your messaging and how you speak about your offers?

Right now, the industry is growing and changing so fast, and there's so much noise in the marketplace. So if you write messaging the same way you did even one year ago, it's going to blend in. You need a unique way of communicating your message so it can land in the body. I call this "Sensory Selling…"

And you'll find that when you apply the Category of One Messaging Method, and use Sensory Selling when you communicate…

You turn boring words into an immersive and memorable brand experience. Now, I don't just wanna teach it to you. I wanna make sure that you actually apply what you learn in this chapter, so I'm going to walk you through applying my Category of One Messaging Method at the end to take your messaging from making some money to making insane money.

But first, I want to show you how it looks in action, and what's on the other side of implementing the Category of One Messaging Method…

HOW ONE VIP DAY WITH ME GAVE HER A $55,000 PER MONTH RAISE

In January, Megan enrolled into my 1:1 VIP Event Consulting Experience. When we started working together, her offer wasn't converting as well as it once did, creating a dip in her income. For context, Megan had already built a six-figure business. She had a stack of client results, reliable sales and marketing systems, she was posting and selling consistently, and investing into high-level mastermind spaces.

She built a community and email list of thousands. However, there was a big disconnect between the number of people opting in and engaging in her community vs. the number of people buying.

Megan was…

- Getting price objections on her $1,397, 3 month coaching program, hearing "that's too expensive." She wanted to raise her rates, but was hesitant because offer sales had slowed
- Wanting to get better at speaking to sell, presenting on video, and inviting her audience into her offer from her weekly livestreams

- Wanting a consistent flow of clients joining her program, without having to chase them or convince them of the value

You know your messaging needs work when clients don't see the value in your offer, or feel like you need to "convince" them to buy.

Megan joined my 1:1 VIP Event Consulting Experience. In this experience, you get access to everything from done-for-you visual branding, to my 1:1 support to create or refine your high-ticket offer, and optimize your marketing and funnels… to the exact virtual or in-person event blueprint (down to what to say & how to launch on the back end of your event to fill your offers) that you can rinse to launch and sell your high-ticket offers while impacting thousands more around the world and leaving attendees remembering your event as "the day that changed everything for them."

We immediately booked her VIP Day, where you get more done in a single day than months in some coaching programs.

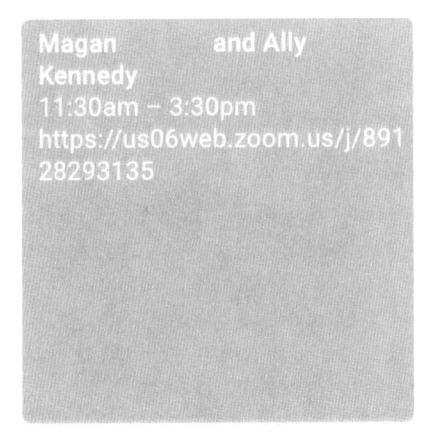

Magan and Ally Kennedy
11:30am – 3:30pm
https://us06web.zoom.us/j/89128293135

Within 20 minutes, I found gaps in her messaging that were leaving thousands of dollars on the table each month. We refined her entire business, starting with the vision for her movement, the identity she was inviting her movement members into, and threaded that into every piece of her business, from her brand, to her messaging, to her marketing and sales strategy.

We...

- Shifted her brand from basic to becoming the vehicle for a movement. We elevated and refined her brand to create an Instant Influence Identity—to be an immediate "YES" to her dream clients
- Refined her signature offer messaging to carry her movement identity. We got clear on her signature method and broke down the micro methods with her process to create "Authority Accelerators" that positioned her as a Category of One.
- Elevated her messaging to speak to clients who were ready to buy. We refined the promise and tangible results of her offer to speak to the benefits and transformation, rather than the features included in the offer. Her new messaging was so sexy, her current clients (in the same offer) were asking "What is this new offer?"
- Hosted a series of virtual events, igniting her Influence and propelling her into five-figure launches (having her "best launch ever"). Delivering her events gave her so much clarity on how to present her offer, 10Xing her confidence and conviction on live streams and in sales conversations.

Her goal in January was $100k for the entire year. After our VIP Day, her business skyrocketed, and now, she's aiming for $100K months by December.

It's never been easier to make an income online. However, to make that your reality, you need to be able to clearly articulate the value of your work, and position yourself as a Category of One in your industry.

When you're one of many, you look and sound like other leaders in your industry. When you're a Category of One, you are the diamond of your industry. Rare, unique, extremely valuable.

To help these concepts land, I want to show you the before and after of Megan's offer so you can see how she applied the Category of One

Message Method, before I walk you through the framework, so you can do the same.

BEFORE APPLYING THE CATEGORY OF ONE MESSAGING METHOD

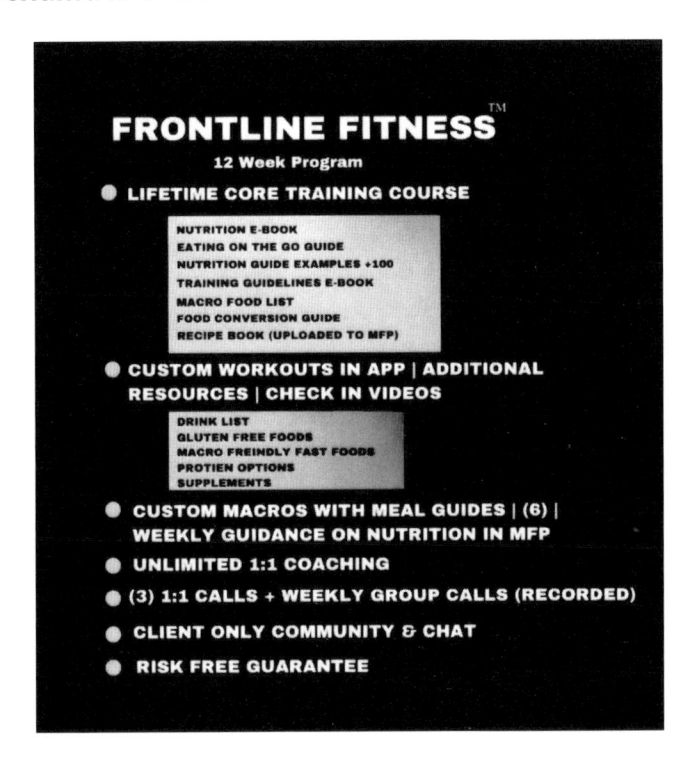

```
FRONTLINE FITNESS™
12 Week Program
● LIFETIME CORE TRAINING COURSE
    NUTRITION E-BOOK
    EATING ON THE GO GUIDE
    NUTRITION GUIDE EXAMPLES +100
    TRAINING GUIDELINES E-BOOK
    MACRO FOOD LIST
    FOOD CONVERSION GUIDE
    RECIPE BOOK (UPLOADED TO MFP)
● CUSTOM WORKOUTS IN APP | ADDITIONAL
   RESOURCES | CHECK IN VIDEOS
    DRINK LIST
    GLUTEN FREE FOODS
    MACRO FREINDLY FAST FOODS
    PROTIEN OPTIONS
    SUPPLEMENTS
● CUSTOM MACROS WITH MEAL GUIDES | (6) |
   WEEKLY GUIDANCE ON NUTRITION IN MFP
● UNLIMITED 1:1 COACHING
● (3) 1:1 CALLS + WEEKLY GROUP CALLS (RECORDED)
● CLIENT ONLY COMMUNITY & CHAT
● RISK FREE GUARANTEE
```

Before we worked on Megan's offer, she was making the most common mistakes I see coaches make when they talk about their offers. She was listing the features (aka the "stuff" - calls, community, coaching, etc.) included with her program.

The problem with this?

High-ticket buyers don't want calls, community, coaching, etc. They want the results on the other side of them.

Now, I want to show you the copy I wrote for her new offer, after applying the Category of One Messaging Method...

AFTER APPLYING THE CATEGORY OF ONE MESSAGING METHOD

Fit Frontliner™ Elite Partnership Program

In 4 Months you'll have all of the elements (mindset, nutrition, fitness plan) personalized to YOUR unique lifestyle, schedule, & what equipment you have available to help you burn fat, lose 3-5 inches from your waist & 10-40lbs... WHILE increasing energy & feeling stronger, more rested, more confident, happy in your own skin...and feeling like a total BADASS when you look in the mirror...

In the most effective way possible, so you can get twice the results in half the time. But more importantly, in a way that's sustainable, so you can get and KEEP the results you want.

Frontline Fitness Formula™

I'm basically giving you a shortcut to the body, energy levels & results you want... done for you... 0 thinking required. A customized roadmap, responsible for helping my clients kick ass, feel great & losing up to 40 lbs in 16 weeks. You'll think, "I never knew weight loss could be this easy..." because I've already done the work for you!

Fat Burner Blueprint™

Secrets of losing 3-5 inches from your waist & 10-40 lbs in 16 weeks

A unique macro, meal guide & nutrition blueprint tailored to your body, lifestyle, and activity levels to help you lose fat & shed weight. Within a few short weeks, you'll be hearing, "You look amazing, are you doing something different?" The cool part is we start with a baseline of what you're eating right now & tweak your diet to hit your macros & goals without getting bored or giving up foods or drinks you love. (My meal guide even has wine lol)

The 20 Minute Body Bundle™

Workouts customized to get you results in as little as 20 min a day or less

You don't need hours in a gym to burn fat, look and feel incredible, and create the body you want in 20 minutes. We'll map out your body bundle based on time, & equipment available. That way you start seeing noticeable toning and slimming all over... without having to worry about finding equipment at the gym. You'll feel stronger, more comfortable in your body, and think "WOW... I didn't know my body could look like THIS..." when you look in the mirror.

Fit for Life Formula™

To help you get results & KEEP THEM, even after the program

I'm going to teach you how to maintain long-term health & fitness success. You'll receive ebook updates, new success plans, and mindset tips even after your time in the program ends, so you can build your own workouts, stay on top of your nutrition, and stay accountable even after the program is done.

Let's break down the major differences in the updated offer and copy that created an explosion of clients and income in Megan's business...

When crafting the new copy for the Fit Frontliner™ Elite Partnership Program offer, I made sure to...

- Turn her offer into the vehicle for a movement by giving it a name that is benefit driven and speaks to the future identity her clients desire.
- Present her Unique Methodology and every "Micro Method" or step she takes her clients through to get results in a way that is benefit driven and speaks to the transformation
- Highlight how her method was different from what her clients may have seen before or tried before to lose weight
- Use ultra specificity when describing the tangible outcomes of her offer, using numbers, dates, and times
- Use Sensory Selling, describing to how the offer would make them feel, what they would be thinking, and what they would hear from others they interacted with as a result of the program, so they could envision themselves in their future reality

The biggest takeaways?

1) People don't buy products or services. They buy the problems they solve. They buy who they become on the other side of them.

2) High-ticket clients want results. The faster and easier you can deliver those results, and the more unique your process of getting the results, the more valuable your offer becomes. When you understand how to speak about your work in a way that allows buyers to visualize using the product, even without physically seeing it, your sales will skyrocket.

Now, I want to walk you through how you can apply the most impactful pieces of the Category of One Messaging Method to your offers, so you can stand out as the obvious choice in your industry, and fill your $2,000-$20,000 offers with dream clients.

JANUARY 2024, $5,000 MONTHS

> What Is Your Average Monthly Business Revenue over the past 6 months?
> 5000

JULY 2024, $60,000 MONTHS

> Sorry I've been swamped. I've been signing about +5 clients per week
>
> is to bring on another coach bc I'm at 30 clients right now this month so I'll have to train them too. Bc I'm expecting another 5-10 clients by the end of the month
>
> Bruh I'm aiming for 100k by Dec easily

THESE MESSAGING SHIFTS THAT WILL ADD THOUSANDS TO YOUR INCOME EVERY MONTH

I work with our Wealthy Woman Society VIP Mastermind members and one on one clients on their Category of One messaging, just like I did for Megan on our VIP day. For the sake of this book, I'm going to cover a few of the most important pieces of the Category of One messaging method that you can apply to your own to skyrocket your sales. Crafting your messaging is simple. Anyone can do it. It's a learned skill. And once you nail it? Signing high-paying clients on repeat is easy.

I'm going to break some messaging concepts down that you've likely never heard presented in this way. At the end of the chapter, you're going to workshop them, and implement them in your own business. And in the next chapter, we're going to talk about how to amplify your message with speaking, so you can impact thousands more, and fill your high-ticket offers on the spot from your virtual and in-person events.

One of the most important pieces of your messaging is how you position your **Unique Methodology** as a new way for your clients to get results. New isn't just a fancy wrapper. New = hope. Hope that what you're offering will finally be the solution your dream client has been searching for.

The name should be benefit driven, making it immediately clear what result your clients will get on the other side. Call this your XYZ SYSTEM, XYZ BLUEPRINT, XYZ FORMULA, XYZ METHOD.

Examples: *The Wealthy Woman Way, Bombshell Blueprint, Soulful Business Blueprint, Frontline Fitness Formula*

Naming your Unique Methodology is where most mentors stop, but I'm not most mentors…

THERE ARE TWO SALES YOU NEED TO MAKE

When you're speaking about your work, there are two sales you need to make. You need to get your audience bought in on your process before they're bought in on your product. The key here is to thread the Micro Methods of your process to how your dream clients actually want to experience the results.

For example, when I wrote the copy for Megan's Fit Frontliner™ Elite Partnership Program offer, I knew her ideal clients were busy frontline workers who were typically working 12-16 hour shifts, or working on the road all day in a vehicle. I highlighted pieces of the Frontline Fitness Formula in a way that speaks to the experience of getting results that her clients care about, including…

- Personalized to your unique lifestyle, schedule, and what equipment you have available
- In the most effective way possible, so you can get twice the results in half the time
- Workouts customized to get you results in as little as 20 min a day or less
- Without getting bored or giving up foods or drinks you love
- Get results and __keep them__, even after the program

We positioned her offer against the fitness gurus who make you work out for 60 minutes, spend hours meal prepping, and make you give up all the foods you love… causing you to gain the weight back immediately after your program ends because the plan they gave you was not sustainable for your lifestyle. As a result? Her offer exploded with clients.

Right now, you're assuming clients know what to expect in your process. However, they don't know what's on the other side of their purchase, so they're sitting on the fence waiting to hire you. Speaking to results like "Weight Loss" or "Make Money" is one of many messaging mistakes in today's market.

When you're able to articulate your process in a way that's new, unique, different, and speaks to the *experience* your clients want to have on the way to the results... you'll become a Category of One, and explode the number of clients in your high-ticket offers.

It's kinda like if you want your client to book a first class flight. You don't show them a picture of the outside of the plane, or the inner workings of a Boeing 747. You show them people sipping champagne, relaxing with pillows in their spacious seats, and enjoying the ride to their dream destination.

Now, let's name your **Micro Methods**, a.k.a. the steps that you take your clients through to get them results. Give each step a sexy name that speaks to the result of that step.

When you name your Micro Methods, you create what I call Authority Acceleration Content. Authority Acceleration Content collapses time building trust and certainty with your audience because it **1) shifts the process you take your clients through from one of many to Category of One 2) Positions your solution as new, unique, and different than anything they've heard before or tried before. Rarity adds value.**

Examples: *Instant Influence Identity, Category of One Messaging, Six Figure Speaker System, Wealthy Speaker Roadmap, Fat Burner Blueprint, The 20 Minute Body Bundle, Fit for Life Formula*

CLIENTS PAY BIG WHEN THEY FEEL UNDERSTOOD

People do not need to understand you to buy, they need to know you understand them.

To show them you understand, I want you to think about the problem your offer solves. Now, think about going through an entire day as your ideal client living with that problem. How does the problem show up in their life day-to-day? This is how you create **Ultra Specific Micro Symptoms** of the Problem.

From here, you want to describe the micro experiences she desires within the macro result.

When you articulate your dream client's problems and solutions with this level of granularity, they will think "wow, she's in my head..." when they read it, they will join any offer, at any price, without needing a sales call or 100 DMs.

Example of problem: Signing on some high-ticket clients, know they should be signing on way more

Examples of Ultra Specific Micro Symptoms of the problem: Hearing "that's too expensive," "I'll think about it," or "maybe next time" when you drop the price. People asking for the link, and not buying. Getting ghosted in the DMs after you drop a price.

Examples of Micro Solutions it provides: Hearing "F*CK YES! I'm in!" when you send the price of your highest ticket offer, every person who asks for the link buys because you're only attracting people who are ready to buy

When speaking to your Micro Solutions, remember that the speed of results is the new size of results. The faster you can get results, the more valuable your offer becomes. Think: how can you adjust the delivery of your offer to get results faster?

Finally, what are your dream clients thinking, feeling, hearing, experiencing? Imagine yourself in the scenario of the Micro Symptom you just described. Your goal is to dimensionalize this experience. You can do this using…

- What they are feeling
- What others are saying to them
- What they are thinking
- What they are saying to others
- What other sensations they are experiencing in their body

When you layer in these steps, you take your message from one of many to Category of One.

You will fill your $2k-$20k+ offers from content alone when…

- Every post, story, email you share speaks directly to your dream client
- You stop trying to "show value" and start showing your high-value solutions to high-value problems
- You speak to the high-value micro-ultra-specificity of your work
- You understand she doesn't care about your results as much as she cares about hers.

When you nail your Category of One Messaging… you don't just stand out as the obvious choice in your industry… you are the industry.

Now it's your turn to give yourself a $55,000 per month raise, like Megan did, by applying the Category of One Messaging method to your messaging.

In the next chapter, I'm going to show you how to bring this message to life in a way that impacts millions around the world and collapse your monthly income into a day using your voice.

HOMEWORK

- What is the name of your Unique Method? What is the problem it solves?
- What are the Micro Methods (aka the steps) you take your clients through to get results? List out your offer framework and the steps you take to get your clients results. Give them sexy, benefit driven names. Get specific on how your Micro Methods deliver on the experience of getting results that your clients care about.
- What are the Ultra Specific Micro Symptoms of the Problem? How does this problem show up in day-to-day life for your dream client? What scenarios do they experience because of it?
- What are the Ultra Specific Micro Solutions of the Problem? How do these results look in the day-to-day life for your

dream client? What positive scenarios do they experience because of the result you've gotten them?
- What are they thinking, feeling, hearing, experiencing as a result of your Unique Method, and each Micro Method you take them through?

Name of Unique Method:	Ultra Specific Micro Problems	Micro Solutions it Provides	What are they thinking, feeling, hearing, experiencing as a result?
Step 1 Micro Method Name:			
Step 2 Micro Method Name:			
Step 3 Micro Method Name:			

SPEAK TO SELL YOUR HIGH-TICKET OFFERS

"Ally, can you share in the group that you're there for them if they need help with support with speech that they can hire you? You are the ONLY person I endorse for this."

My eyes filled with tears.

I just parked at the coffee shop to grab my daily iced oat milk latte.

And I opened my telegram to see this...

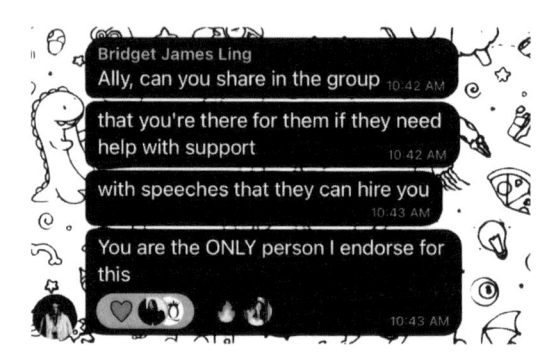

> **Bridget James Ling**
> Ally, can you share in the group 10:42 AM
>
> that you're there for them if they need help with support 10:42 AM
>
> with speeches that they can hire you 10:43 AM
>
> You are the ONLY person I endorse for this
> 10:43 AM

It was a message from Bridget James Ling.

She hired me to EmCee her conference, Freedom Queen Live.

And now, she was giving me permission to offer my In the Arena one on-one speaking mentorship packages to her speakers.

In fact, she went as far to tell her speakers that I am the *only* person she endorses for them to hire.

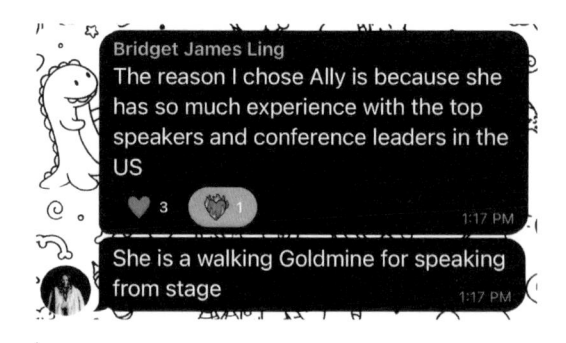

> **Bridget James Ling**
> The reason I chose Ally is because she has so much experience with the top speakers and conference leaders in the US
> ♥ 3   1:17 PM
>
> She is a walking Goldmine for speaking from stage 1:17 PM

Why do I tell you this?

Because not all speaking is created equal.

When most people think of speaking, they think of keynotes and TED Talks.

Speaking to sell isn't just selling from a stage or an event. Speaking to sell is a way of communicating with someone. It's understanding the art of influence and persuasion. When do you do it well? They buy your product or service.

Right now, if you…

- Post content daily
- Sell your offers daily
- Go live on social media
- Host a podcast
- Host a masterclass
- Host a virtual event
- Host an in-person event
- Sell in the DMs

You are already speaking to sell.

And when you look at the top names in the industry? They're all speaking to sell, and using events to fill their high-ticket offers on the spot (which I'll show you how to do in the next section).

Because we both know you're meant for more than making some money from content alone. And when it comes to speaking…

Speaking to sell is the best way to impact the most amount of people in the shortest time. Speaking to sell collapses time between people finding your brand and buying your program.

Speaking to sell is the #1 wealth building skill in the world.

Who do you think of when you think of the top speakers in the game, who comes to mind?

Tony Robbins comes to mind first.

Tony Robbins is in his 60s. He won't be in the game that much longer. My vision is to teach you to be the next Tony Robbins in your industry.

Because the reality is, the demand for speakers is higher than the number of speakers in the industry. I have to turn down so many speaking opportunities. I can't take them all. That's why I'm training an army of speakers. So I can place you on stages and match you with our clients who need speakers.

When it comes to sales? You already know sales is the most important skill you need to learn in your business...

So when you fast forward and look back on the years you invested building your business... how do you want to remember your life?

How do you want to remember the impact you made in the world?

Sitting behind a computer?
Glued to social media 24/7?
Living in your office?

Or getting paid to travel the world while witnessing your online business explode... moving the masses with your message, walking off of stages to people running up to you with tears in their eyes, telling you, "Your talk changed my life..."

Because you learned how to speak to sell?

When you know how to speak to sell, **sales gets to be fun.**

People love to buy from you. You will have people coming up to you after you get off stage with their credit cards in hand asking you how they can work with you.

But it's not enough for you to wait for an invitation to speak at a big event where you will get lost in a sea of second-stage faces all trying to pitch their books, courses, and programs to a diverse audience.

Building your own stage, and hosting your own events is the fastest way to attract the type of clients who say, "I want to work with HER," as soon as you step off the stage.

Learning how to speak to sell from is how you will collapse your monthly income into a day using your voice.

When you master speaking to sell… you and your income will become limitless. Your current ceiling will become your new floor. Every part of your business will level up. Your engagement will rise, your conversion rates from every email, post, and story will skyrocket, and this will compound into five- and six-figure days.

You will experience true freedom to sell what you want and live how you want because you know how to sell anything with or without your time and presence. Because you know how to speak to sell one to many, your business is set up to create more space, and you have multiple streams of income coming in from your offers as well as getting paid to speak and travel.

You can see yourself being flown out, all expenses paid, to speak at massive events in your industry, impacting thousands more through your work. Being one of "THE GREATS" in your industry.

You can see yourself hosting your own virtual and in-person events. Turning social media into your stage. Moving people to tears in a Zoom room. Receiving DMs for weeks from dream clients saying, "I'm still having breakthroughs… your event changed everything for me."

In the upcoming chapters, I'm going to walk you through step-by-step, how to 10X your impact while 10X-ing your income speaking to sell.

FROM PRICE OBJECTIONS ON A $4,000 OFFER TO CLIENTS JOINING HER $12,000 OFFER WITHIN MINUTES OF DROPPING IT FROM HER EVENT

Focusing on sales and marketing alone will keep you plateaued, because people don't just hire you to solve their problems.

They hire you for *who you are*.
They hire you for *how you lead*.
They hire you for *the way you make them feel*.

Only thinking about "What to do"? That's an energetic match for minimum wage.

You get paid because of *who you are*. Your high-level, high-paying dream clients don't want information. They want leadership. They *feel* that. They wanna be beside that. They pay anything for that.

This is embodiment.

Your income has no limit when your leadership and embodiment has no limit.

There are a lot of people teaching "sell on Instagram stories," "just post content," and "steal my 4 phase launch plan…" But there are millions of other marketers using the same strategies.

What will set *you* apart (which is what most business mentors fail to mention) is when you *also* master…

- How to lead a room
- How to communicate with influence
- How to turn your body of work into an experience
- How to speak in a way that changes lives (and creates clients)

What will set you apart is learning how to speak to sell your high-ticket offers. Speaking to sell your high-ticket offers is the ultimate way to continue to rise to new levels in your leadership and embodiment.

And when you combine this level of who to be with a proven strategy for launching and selling your offers from virtual and in-person events (which I'll walk you through in the next chapter)... **your brand and business will take off.**

Just like my client Donna's did.

In February, Donna messaged me to chat about 1:1 VIP Event Consulting. We had a couple quick conversations. She filled out the application. Within days of our initial conversation she was paid in full & ready to go.

> ALLY!!!! We want to benefit from your brilliance and your conference program. Let us know our next steps! Xoxox Amber and DMC

She consciously chose to invest in a space that didn't "make sense" based on where she currently was... **but made *perfect sense* based on where she wanted to go.**

When she came in, she had already built a multi-six figure business. She was a leader in her industry and author of three books. The moment I met her, I told her, "You're basically famous." I knew she was meant to be an Industry Icon.

However, she was experiencing some resistance in her business. Her offer was starting to fatigue, and although it had a track record of converting well, she was starting to get price objections on her $4,000 signature offer. She felt frustrated because she knew she was meant for so much more than *just* sales and marketing. She wanted to impact women around the world, and she was ready to host the leading event to make that her reality.

She was ready to get in the room with a mentor who challenged her to think bigger, helped her remember who the f*ck she is, held the mirror up to remind of her power, and could help her turn her business into the vehicle for a global movement.

In a single VIP day, we mapped out her vision for the Sister Leader movement, her new mastermind offer that highlighted her zone of genius, and her conference launch strategy, from the marketing message, down to what to say in the room to fill her offer.

We do more in a single VIP day than 6 months in most coaching programs. This was Donna's response after we finished...

> And then there's Ally overdelivering like a BOSS!

> That was mind-blowing honestly

She raised her standards, elevated the type of client she wanted to serve, elevated her messaging to create a Category of One in her industry, her visuals to craft a High End Brand with an Instant Influence Identity, and her leadership to match the new level of client she wanted to call in.

She shifted from building a business to igniting a global movement. She claimed her offer as the BEST offer on the internet streets...

And her event was the BEST F*CKING EVENT IN THE WORLD.

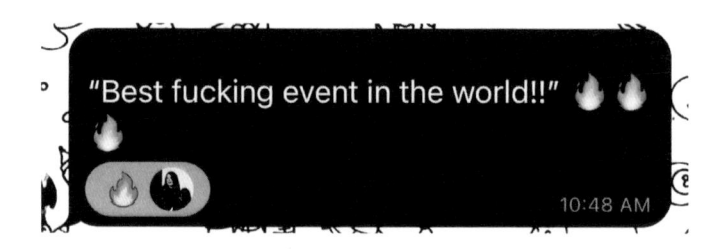

> "Best fucking event in the world!!"
>
> 10:48 AM

She leaned into mentorship. Showed up for every call. Implemented the coaching immediately. She was inside our one-on-one Telegram chat almost every day taking massive action and asking for feedback. She celebrated every step of the journey.

If something felt "off," she immediately leaned in for support, a set of eyes on her marketing, a shift in her launch plan, or an activation to help her remember who the F*ck she was. She is receptive to being "loved & shoved" and called to rise to a higher standard than she would hold herself... A standard we both knew she was born to operate at... but she was still building belief around.

Here's the thing, Ally believed in me more than I believed in myself as we planned this amazing event.

She knew she wanted more than *just* another group program or mastermind.

She went all in on a space where she had 1:1 support on every piece of strategy as well as the mindset and energetics to activate it. A mentor who was in the arena at every virtual and in-person event. A space where she had access to creative direction and an in-house design team. White glove treatment.

She didn't let her current reality or current income level define where she was going. She built her own stage. She made moves based on where she wanted to go. She was willing to take courageous action & make BOLD moves if it meant she was going to leap in her impact, influence, and multiply her income.

And that's exactly why she's become the woman whose clients fly from around the world to get in the room without batting an eyelash & investing to work with her at 3X her original rate. When she dropped her brand new $12,000 offer from the stage, women were running to join the offer within minutes of her dropping it.

Saying "YES" to building her own stage for her conference ignited a fire within Donna. She went from playing it "safe..." to becoming audacious about who she is and what she wants to be known for. She claimed her space as the one in her industry, and 10X'd her conviction in selling. This blew up her brand, visibility & influence like crazy... and her sales multiplied because of it.

Today?

Donna Marie's newest program is sold out months in advance. She's getting paid to speak on stages around the world. She just messaged our group chat today saying she landed a $2,500 paid speaking gig.

> Just closed 2500 speaking fee for a one day event in Washington state in may. 150-200 female admins

And sure, having one-on-one support to install the Six Figure Speaker system (which you'll walk through step-by-step in the next chapter) into her business was the linchpin for skyrocketing her success with speaking...

However, it wasn't just the strategy that blew up Donna's business.

Donna became the woman people love to buy high-ticket offers from by embodying Super Sexy Sales energy. You're probably wondering... "What is Super Sexy Sales energy?"

Let me break it down for you now before I walk you step-by-step through your own virtual or in-person event launch in the next chapter.

HOW TO BECOME THE WOMAN PEOPLE LOVE TO BUY HIGH-TICKET OFFERS FROM

"SEXY AF."

That was the message she sent me right before she paid in full for my high-ticket offer.

Only an hour before, I received an inquiry from an industry leader who reached out for support crafting an upcoming talk she was delivering at an in-person event.

> Hi my queen!! How are you? Do you have any capacity to help me with my speech and if so what would that look like? 🔥🔥🔥
>
> 8:53 AM

This woman is a powerhouse, and she's known for sales and leadership.

I approached the conversation like I would with anyone else. Asking a few questions to make sure I could help her, and if so, prescribe the right solution to move her in the direction of her goals.

We figured out that the In the Arena one on one speaker training experience was the best fit, and right before she paid in full to join this high-ticket experience, she sent this message…

> PS. I looooove way you sell 😉 11:37 AM
>
> SEXY AF 🔥
> 11:37 AM

Why do I tell you this story?

Speaking to sell isn't just selling from a stage or an event. Speaking to sell is understanding communication principles. When you do it well, people buy your product or service and it feels like butter on the nervous system for the buyer and the seller.

Your audience WANTS to be sold to.

They WANT growth. They WANT expansion. They want to access your wisdom and magic. They WANT the transformation only you can provide.

Your ideal client is like a sexy, emotionally available, successful, single man who is searching for someone exactly like YOU to partner with and create their dream life. So what do you do? You embody Super Sexy Sales Energy.

What is Super Sexy Sales Energy?

This is the energy you bring when you have a Super Sexy High-Ticket Offer (which I show you step-by-step how to create inside of Six Figure Speaker). When you embody this level of certainty in your offer, and know you've positioned your offer to deliver on your dream client's desires… (aka the two biggest factors your clients need to make an empowered purchasing decision)… It's kinda like being the hottest girl at a bar. You know all the guys are looking at you. You know you've got it goin' on. You know everybody wants what you have.

The energy in sales is no different. When you work with me to create your Super Sexy High-Ticket Offer, you know your offer is the hottest thing on the internet streets. So when you speak to sell, whether that's from stage at your event, or in the DMs with a dream client, you're grounded in your certainty. You're not attached to the sale, so you divorce yourself from the outcome. And when you show up to sell? You….

- Sell like you know everyone is gonna buy
- Sell like you already have multi millions in your bank account

- Sell like you have all the evidence in the world
- Sell like you know it's gonna work and there's not much else you have to say
- Sell like your offer is the hottest on the internet streets (because *it is*)
- Sell like it's such a no brainer
- Sell like everyone should buy your offer (because *they should*)
- Sell like your best launch ever already happened, it's already done

The level of leadership and certainty you step into when you speak to sell is what helps you become the woman that people love to buy high-ticket offers from.

Sales conversations, whether it's one to one in the DMs, or one to many from your virtual or in-person events, feel as easy as breathing for you when you know how to speak to sell in a way that attracts empowered clients who are ready to buy.

Multiplying the number of clients reaching out to you, because you are the non-negotiable choice in your industry to hire, is the byproduct of who you'll become after you implement the Six Figure Speaker System.

In the next chapter, I'll walk you through it step-by-step so you can launch your next virtual or in-person event.

HOMEWORK

- What do you desire to be known for? What is the one word you want people to hear and immediately think of your name? (Example: Speaking) When you look at your social media, is it obvious that this is the topic you are known for?
- Are you currently speaking or hosting virtual or in-person events on this topic? If no, why not? If yes, how can you get louder or more audacious about who you are and what you do? How can you innovate and bring a fresh angle to how you present your topic to the world?

- Are you positioning yourself as a specialist by selling offers on the topic you want to be known for? Or are you diluting your authority and selling offers around a bunch of other topics as well? (Hint: when you want to be known for everything you won't be known for anything.)
- What needs to be cleaned up in the focal point of your brand, message, what you're speaking on, and the types of offers you're selling, to create a stronger perception as the go-to authority on the topic you want to be known for?

III: SIX FIGURE SPEAKER SYSTEM

HOW TO HOST EVENTS THAT IMPACT MILLIONS WORLDWIDE AND COLLAPSE YOUR MONTHLY INCOME INTO A DAY

"When your identity is limitless, your income is limitless."
—Ally Kennedy

"Yeah, but that's not possible for me..."

Do you ever find yourself thinking this when you see other women celebrating massive wins?

Over the next few chapters, I'm going to show you how to collapse your monthly income into a day speaking to sell from virtual and in-person events. But before I show you how to do that, I want to help you shift your mindset... Because right now, you don't believe you can collapse your monthly income into a day.

When you see people say "I had a $100,000 day!" Your mind goes... "yeah, that happens for her because she has a huge audience, but it doesn't happen for me."

The reason you have these thoughts is because you identify as someone who these results are far away from. Whether you realize it or not, you've created an identity around your current level of income. Even if you're making great money right now... you identify with, "I make $20k months," or, "I make $50K months..." And that's exactly why you've been making $20k or $50k months for months, even years, and you haven't broken that glass ceiling.

The reason you haven't jumped to your next level of income is because your identity is based on the label you're giving yourself. So when you tell yourself "I'm someone who makes $20k months..." You are labeling yourself.

And that label?

That is where your actions are capped. That is where your power is capped. And you're making the amount of money in alignment with the limited mindset that is capped at the identity which you've labeled yourself.

For you to collapse your monthly income into a day, you need to tap into your Limitless Wealth Identity.

This looks like shifting into a mindset of possibility around your income. When you shift into your Limitless Wealth Identity, you think…

- "Insane money is my norm."
- "Anything can happen today."
- "I can make any amount of money today."
- "It doesn't matter how much money I made yesterday, anything can happen today."
- "It doesn't matter how much money I made last month, anything can happen this month."
- "It doesn't matter how many people are watching, I can make any amount of money I want to make."

When you shift into your Limitless Wealth Identity, you are open to the possibility of being blown away by your results every day.

When you shift into your Limitless Wealth Identity, your past results don't determine your current results. When you shift into your Limitless Wealth Identity, anything can happen at any moment. When your identity is limitless, your income is limitless.

Having a Limitless Wealth Identity makes collapsing your monthly income into a day possible.

So what would it look like for you to take on the possibility that collapsing your monthly income into a day can happen for you right now? What if you got curious and said…

"Who is the version of me that collapses her monthly income into a day? "Who is the version of me that makes multi five-figure… even six-figure days?"

The first step to collapsing your monthly income into a day is to shift out of the identity you've created around your current level of income, and shift into your Limitless Wealth Identity.

From there, you will align your actions, energy, and belief system with this new identity.

In the next few chapters, I'm going to show you how to build on this concept with the strategy to collapse your monthly income into a day using your voice.

By the end of this section, you'll be launching your next event.

HOMEWORK

- Think about the version of you who is tapped into her Limitless Wealth Identity and makes multi five-figures... even six-figures in a single day. List 5-10 of her characteristics.

Characteristic:_____ Rating: ___ /10

Characteristic:_____ Rating: ___ /10

Characteristic:_____ Rating: ___ /10

Characteristic:_____ Rating: ___ /10

Characteristic:_____ Rating: ___ /10

Characteristic:_____ Rating: ___ /10

Characteristic:_____ Rating: ___ /10

Characteristic:_____ Rating: ___ /10

Characteristic:_____ Rating: ___ /10

Characteristic:_____ Rating: ___ /10

- Rate yourself on a scale of 1/10 (no 5s or 7s) on how well you embody these characteristics. What's actually stopping you from showing up as her right now? What shifts can you make today to embody more of these characteristics today?
- What does your mindset, energy, and identity look like when you tap into your Limitless Wealth Identity and embody the characteristics you listed above?

- What do your new daily actions look like when you tap into your Limitless Wealth Identity and embody the characteristics you listed above? Describe a day in the life of that version of you, the one who makes six-figures (or more) in a day.

HOW SHE MADE $100,000 IN A SINGLE WEEKEND WITH 12 PEOPLE IN THE ROOM FOR HER IN-PERSON EVENT

"We can book your travel on your behalf …"

I felt like a rockstar reading the email coming through from my 1:1 VIP Event Consulting client, Amanda.

I work with a lot of high profile clients, but I still get excited by the fact that my clients book my flights and hotels.

I was going to speak at her event and help her sell her high-ticket offer from the stage, and we were preparing behind the scenes to bring the experience to life.

Amanda had a fire offer. She already built a seven-figure business. Making money was as easy as breathing for her.

But when she dropped the offer invitation at her event, some people were buying…But they were not clutching their purses, whipping out their credit cards, and running to buy on the spot.

She didn't know why… But I did.

And it was the same reason why your events are making you some money, but they're not making you insane money. Right now, you have zero problem filling your events. People are flocking from all over the world… investing hundreds, even thousands of dollars to get in the room with you.

When you host an event…You have hundreds of people signing up within a few days… And in person? It's not uncommon for them to fly from around the world to get in the physical room with you. And you know you're delivering a world class experience, because your DMs are filled with…

"I LOVED your event!"
"Thank you so much for creating this experience!"
"This was the best event ever!"

But when you drop your offer invitation?

You make some sales… But your offer isn't converting like crazy. The reason why? It's because you're over teaching and forgetting the most important piece of sales speaking…

People buy when they feel like buying. Your job is to shift the way people feel because of your event.

Your job is to create epiphanies, transformations, and breakthroughs that have your attendees say… "This event changed my life…" AND *think*… "I NEED to be inside this offer…"

This is why I teach my clients how to use Story Selling to Structures (which you'll get a taste of in the upcoming chapters) in their content to create their own epiphanies, transformations, and breakthroughs, in a way that adds certainty and trust (aka what your attendees need to make an empowered buying decision), so you attendees see your offer as the only solution.

Story Selling to Structures will create the foundations of a transformational event, but it's not what makes people think, "I need this NOW" when you drop an offer. That's where the Fast Buyer Framework comes in.

The Fast Buyer Framework are the sales speaking techniques to weave into your Story Selling Structures that create an internal momentum that has attendees pulling their credit card out faster than you can say "Pay in Full" the moment you drop an offer. I break the Fast Buyer Framework down step-by-step inside of Six Figure Speaker.

My superpower is that I can spot the exact gaps in your event content and invitation strategy that are keeping you from having multi-five, even six-figure + days on repeat...

Just like I did with my client in 30 minutes.

After day two of her event, we went over the program invitation she delivered, and I told her where the gaps were in the invitation. I told her exactly why more people weren't moving.

So we crafted a new invitation, selling her audience on their future identity, speaking to high-value micro problems and high-value micro solutions, just like you did in your Category of One Message Method. We use a handful of techniques from the Fast Buyer Framework to deliver the new invitation, painting the vision of how their life would feel on the other side of the transformation of her offer.

The result?

We implemented the exact plan in the re-pitch the following day, adding $70,000 to her event sales over the next day. The refinements we made and implemented during that 30-minute meeting brought six-figures in sales in a single weekend from her in-person event.

> Y'all... I just finished hosting my event with the incredible @Ally Kennedy live and in-person. We *averaged* $4900 per attendee in revenue closed, and closed 69% of the room this weekend. Already sold 40% of the room to our next event in 6 mos. We're still doing follow-up, so let's keep going... more is on the table for a 6-figure weekend, we're working that process!

The cool part?

She only had 12 people in the room.

You do not need a big room to make a lot of money from your event. You just need to decide you are a speaker, build your own stage, and be willing to lead the room.

We both know that you're not here to make money from content... You're a trendsetter, an Industry Icon, here to make a huge impact with your message speaking from stages, hosting epic events around the world.

Over the next few chapters, I'm going to walk you through the Six Figure Speaker System and show you step-by-step how to launch your next virtual or in-person event, so you can make this your story.

BEING SOLD TO AT AN EVENT CHANGED MY LIFE

"If you guys never sold the mastermind at that event, I wouldn't be having this conversation with you right now."

I was on a call with one of the partners of Clients and Community, an eight-figure coaching company, who have helped their clients do over $150 Million in revenue.

I just landed the biggest speaking gig of my career, landing a $10,000 contract (with my flight and luxury hotel included on top of that) to speak on one of the top stages in my industry...

And I was getting some great tips from his experience hosting multiple sales events. It was normal for these events to bring in a minimum of a quarter of a million dollars in a single weekend.

When we ended the call, my eyes filled up with tears when I told him...

"Thank you for selling to me at that event. These events changed my life and business forever."

Trust is...

If they never sold me a $24,000 mastermind at that event, you would not be reading *Speak Your Way to Wealth* right now.

If they never sold me a $24,000 mastermind at that event, I would have never bought that $49 mic from Amazon and started hosting events in the common room of my apartment.

If they never sold me a $24,000 mastermind at that event, the Wealthy Woman Movement would not exist today, and we would not have impacted thousands of women around the globe.

I joined the mastermind and the monthly payments were 2.5X what I was making per month at the time. It didn't make sense... but I bought that offer because I was in my power. I trusted in myself that I was going to make it work... and I did.

Within the first month, I made one third of the entire investment back.

Why?

Because I went all in. Because investing $24,000 stretched me. It demanded that I rise into a new level of leadership. And who I became because of that investment changed my life and business forever.

Right now, if you assume people in your audience can't afford to join your high-ticket offers, what you're really saying is, "I don't believe in you."

Imagine if they didn't sell me that offer because they thought I "couldn't afford it" when I was making just $1,000 per month. Imagine if they said, "she's not ready..." and they didn't let me buy.

If you have an offer or service that can change someone's life, how dare you not sell your high-ticket offers to them because you're projecting your own money beliefs onto them.

Being sold to at that event changed my life...

And now I'm going to show you how you can create the same life-changing opportunities for your attendees by speaking to sell from your events.

THE ULTIMATE WAY TO BUILD AUTHORITY, CREDIBILITY, AND FILL YOUR HIGH-TICKET OFFERS WITH DREAM CLIENTS

Why do events work so well?

Everyone who's been in the room for an event knows there is nothing like it. When you're surrounded by people who are tuned in and turned on…Your chest is buzzing. You get chills when you hear a speaker say something that feels like it was written specifically for you.

There is an energy in the room that can't be replicated.

And sales? **Sales is a transfer of energy.**

Remember how your number one priority is to get in The Wealth Zone, and live there?

Speaking to sell from your own events is how you share that energy with the world. And that energy is what will have your audience immediately think "I want to work with HER…"

So why do I recommend building the stage for your own events?

Because although you can land great speaker fees, you typically can't sell from other people's stages. You will make the most money building your own stage because you can sell high-ticket offers from your events (like I'll show you how to do in this section).

Right now, if your events are filling, but not converting into the number of high-ticket clients you'd like on the backend, it's because you're not being intentional about the structure of your event.

You're…

- Treating your event like a giant masterclass and over-teaching
- Stuffing your event full of guest speakers who are killing your conversions
- Teaching for hours, even days, and then rushing through the invitation because you "don't want it to feel sales-y"
- Not following through with the launch on the back end of you event because you didn't get the number of signups you wanted in the room

Let's fix that once and for all.

Over the next few chapters, I'm going to walk you step-by-step through the Six Figure Speaker System to launch your next virtual or in-person event.

The Six Figure Speaker System is a step-by-step system that ensures you empower millions with your message as you speak to sell out your offers & command the attention of the entire room…no matter how big the audience or what "platform" you're on.

My intention is that the next few chapters bring you massive momentum and results. However, this is only the tip of the iceberg. For the best results, I recommend diving into the Six Figure Speaker Curriculum.

Six Figure Speaker is included when you join the Wealthy Woman Society.

When you join the Wealthy Woman Society from *Speak Your Way to Wealth*, you'll get the exact syntax from our Wealthy Woman Live in-person event, which brings in a minimum of $20,000 in every time we host this intimate, 4-hour mastermind event with as little as 6-10 people in the room.

If you'd like my help with a one-on-one event launch strategy designed to collapse your monthly income into a day, I suggest booking a Speak Your Way to Wealth Virtual VIP Day.

Inside the Speak Your Way to Wealth Virtual VIP Day, you'll craft your signature virtual or in-person event that will get you known around the world for your unique methodology.

You'll leave with the exact event blueprint (down to what to say and how to launch on the back end of your event to fill your offers) that you can rinse and repeat virtually or in-person to launch and sell your high-ticket offers while impacting thousands more around the world, positioning you as an industry icon, and leaving attendees remembering your event as "the day that changed everything for them."

You'll learn to speak to sell your high-ticket offers in a way that has your attendees feel "I want to work with HER," effortlessly filling your $2,000-$20,000 programs as a byproduct.

DM me on Instagram @theallykennedy for details and booking information.

Ok, now let's dive into the Six Figure Speaker System, so that selling out your $2,000-$20,000 offers from your events becomes your new normal.

SIX FIGURE
SPEAKER SYSTEM

SELLING OUT YOUR $2,000-$20,000 OFFERS IS ABOUT TO BECOME YOUR NEW NORMAL.

The Six Figure Speaker System isn't a shortcut... It's a quantum leap.

Making sales on social media isn't new to you... But you're ready to scale your impact and influence even more. You see yourself growing a global movement. You know speaking is your next step in making that happen.

You don't just want to be another "scroll on by" social media profile... you want to be someone who creates an experience of your work. You're already speaking on live streams, podcasts, masterclasses, and you're ready to multiply your current sales across the board...

You're ready to be the woman who commands every room you enter. Your words land like sermons. Your people flock to join your offers. They fly around the world to get in rooms with you... ready to buy every time you open your mouth.

You've been in rooms and you've witnessed how impactful and momentum building speaking is. And instead of continuing to sit in the audience... **you're ready to be the one on the stage.**

You know that speaking to sell is the next evolution of your brand and movement.

You're ready to 10X your impact WHILE 10X-ing your income. You can see yourself being flown out, all expenses paid, to speak at massive events in your industry, impacting millions through your work. You see yourself as one of "The Greats" in your industry. A household name, known for generations to come.

You can see yourself hosting your own virtual and in-person events. Turning social media into your stage. Moving people to tears in a zoom room. Receiving DMs for weeks from dream clients saying, "I'm still having breakthroughs... your event changed everything for me."

Speaking is the fastest and most powerful way to create instant authority and trust. The Six Figure Speaker System helps you...

- Get paid what you really want to
- Leverage your time by selling one-to-many
- Make sales feel light, fun and easy

The Six Figure Speaker System is how you'll collapse your monthly sales into a single day. Our clients have seen results like adding $70,000 in sales in as little as two days, bringing in six-figures in a single weekend, and signing 4-figure pay-in-full clients from as little as 15 minutes of speaking in a zoom room.

The Six Figure Speaker System is responsible for 95% of our recurring revenue and 279% revenue growth from 2022 to 2023 alone... while creating a lifestyle business, getting paid up to five-figures for a single speaking gig to travel and speak from stages around the world.

Here's how it works...

DECIDE

ATTRACT THE RIGHT ATTENDEES FOR YOUR OFFER & HIT YOUR LAUNCH GOALS WITH YOUR VIRTUAL EVENT

First, you need to decide who your ideal attendee is and what you're selling them from your event. Inside **Six Figure Speaker**, I walk you through how to create your own Super Sexy Signature High-Ticket Offer.

The reason we need to begin with the offer in mind is so your event messaging is congruent, and attracts attendees who will be a perfect fit for your offer.

For now, let's walk through the basics of the message you'll need to launch your next profitable event. After that, I'll show you examples of how this messaging comes together.

Who is this for?

- List their positive characteristics
- Who is your event not for?
- What problem are you solving for your ideal attendee?
- What's the payoff you're promising for this customer?
- What's the movement you are inviting them into?

Super Sexy High-Ticket Offer Details

- What is the Name of the offer you'd like to sell at the end of your virtual event?
- What is the primary promise of your offer?
- Name of program
- What's included in the offer stack?
- Offer Price

Event Name

- Event Promise
- Event Pricing
- Event Ticket Pricing

Event Time

- Pick a date to do your event.
- What time does it start?
- Create your ticket offer for the front end of the event.

Now that you've got the basics down, it's time to craft the messaging for your event. To help you do that, I want to show you two examples of events and offer messaging, side by side, so you can get an idea of what this can look like for your event launch.

THE TWO MOST IMPORTANT PIECES OF COPY IN YOUR EVENT LAUNCH

The two most important pieces of copy in your event launch are the offer promise and the event promise. The congruency between the offer promise and the event promise is the sweet spot that aligns your event with your ideal attendee. I'm going to show you two different converting examples from two different industries. But first, here's a template you can swipe and customize to launch your event even faster...

Offer Name + Tagline Template

In one _____(Workshop/Event/Retreat)____ we hold you by the hand and guide you through the __(Core Program Name)__. You'll have all of the elements ____(Pillar 1, Pillar 2, Pillar 3) set up to ____ (Heaven: bright beautiful future and end result)____.

HOW TO HAVE CLIENTS JUMPING INTO YOUR MULTIPLE FIVE-FIGURE MASTERMIND WITHIN MINUTES

The first example I'll walk you through is using our Wealthy Woman Live in-person event to fill our Industry Icon Mastermind. Our goal for the Wealthy Woman Live event was to replicate the experience they would have inside the mastermind. On top of following the Six Figure Speaker System for the event launch, I gave attendees a taste of our curriculum, one on one support in shaping their mini-message, as well as the opportunity to present their mini-message on stage at the event. This was a preview of our one on one in In the Arena Speaker Training, which is included in the Industry Icon mastermind, and is a big differentiator between our mastermind and other business masterminds.

The result?

When we dropped the offer, clients were placing deposits to enroll into the multiple five figure mastermind within minutes. Outside of how you structure your event content (which I'll break down in the next chapter), ask yourself how you can give your attendees a taste of what they will experience in your backend offer.

Here's the exact messaging we used for the event and offer promise to ensure we were attracting ideal attendees into the room who would be a perfect fit for Wealthy Woman Live…

SUPER SEXY HIGH-TICKET OFFER NAME AND PROMISE

Industry Icon

A 12 month mastermind for female coaches and impact driven entrepreneurs to become the woman who can lead a movement and scale your impact, influence, and offers using speaking

By the end of our 12 months together, you'll have all of the elements (offers, events, marketing, visibility, and sales systems) set up to build a six-figure per year (then six-figures per month) business… so you can build a life and business beyond your wildest dreams.

Offer promise breakdown:

What is it? A 12 month mastermind
Who is it for? female coaches and impact driven entrepreneurs
What's the payoff? become the woman who can lead a movement and scale your impact, influence and offers

EVENT NAME AND PROMISE

Wealthy Woman Live: SPEAK

In a single day, you'll leave with your signature offer, talk, and marketing strategy DONE to speak on stages around the globe, launch your next virtual or in-person event, and turn your business into the vehicle for a movement... so you can create the impact (and income) you want in 2024.

Event promise breakdown:

What is it? A single day
Who is it for? female coaches and impact driven entrepreneurs
What's the payoff? Leave with your signature offer

$14,301 LAUNCH WITH HER FIRST VIRTUAL EVENT

When Megan signed on to our VIP Event Consulting experience, she was feeling disconnected from the business model she built. She was burnt out DMing 100s of people a day, and wanted to ditch sales calls in her business. She knew she was meant to make a bigger impact than just selling on social media. Megan wanted to speak. She wanted to host events. She wanted to build a movement. She also wanted to build deeper relationships with her community and turn more of her followers and Facebook group members into clients.

Megan had never hosted an event or spoken publicly outside of weekly live streams in her Facebook group. Her biggest question was, "What do I say on stage?" We worked one on one to craft her event content and implement the Six Figure Speaker System, launching her first ever virtual event, with her brand new offer messaging. Within a few days, she had 123 people signed up (without ads), and made $324 in VIP ticket upgrades before the event even started (Inside Six Figure Speaker, I give you the exact funnel, copy, templates & structures to turn your free attendees into paying customers).

On event day, Megan followed the done-for-you content plan we created for her event (this is included with Six Figure Speaker)... and witnessed her attendees' lives being transformed before her eyes in the room.

The result?

A $14,301 launch... Megan's best launch ever. After the event, she said..."I've never seen that kind of transformation happen on a livestream, sales call, or in a messenger conversation. This is powerful stuff." Here's a breakdown of the virtual event messaging we used to attract ideal attendees who would be the best fit for the Fit Frontliner™ Elite Partnership Program...

OFFER NAME AND PROMISE

Fit Frontliner™ Elite Partnership Program

In 4 months, you'll have all of the elements (mindset, nutrition, fitness plan) personalized to YOUR unique lifestyle, schedule, & what equipment you have available to help you burn fat, lose 3-5 inches from your waist & 10-40lbs... WHILE increasing energy and feeling stronger, more rested, more confident, happy in your own skin...and feeling like a total BADASS when you look in the mirror... in the most effective way possible, so you can get twice the results in half the time. But more importantly, in a way that's sustainable, so you can get and KEEP the results you want.

Offer promise breakdown:

What is it? 4 month program
Who is it for? Frontline Workers and Medical Professionals
What's the payoff? burn fat, lose 3-5 inches from your waist & 10-40lbs

EVENT NAME AND TAGLINE

Fit Frontliner Workshop

A 1-Day Workshop for Frontline Workers & Medical Professionals

By the end of this workshop you'll discover… How my clients are kicking ass, feeling X, & Losing up to 40 lbs in 14 weeks using the Frontline Fitness Formula …even if you work 12 hour shifts, have rotating schedules & you're on the road in a vehicle all day / feel like you have "no time" to do it all

Event promise breakdown:

What is it? A 1 Day Workshop
Who is it for? Frontline Workers & Medical Professionals
What's the payoff? Losing up to 40 lbs in 14 weeks

You don't need to host an in-person event, have any experience as a speaker, or hosting an event… period, to have a successful event launch with the Six Figure Speaker System. Leading her first event ignited a new wave of conviction in the value of her work. She reconnected with why she does what she does, and started showing up in a bigger way in her business because of it.

Within four months of Megan's first virtual event, I opened our one on one chat to see a message from Megan. It read…

"I've been signing about 5 clients per week these past 3-4 weeks…"

Her business was taking off. She went from getting price objections and barely hitting $5,000 months, to tripling her prices, and hitting consistent $60,000. Best part? Megan didn't change her offer. We simply applied the Category of One Message Method you learned in section two of Speak Your Way to Wealth.

Now it's your turn to create your Six Figure Speaker System success story. After you craft your event messaging below, I'll be showing you how to fill your event with ideal attendees.

HOMEWORK

- Who is your event for?
- What is the name and primary promise of the Super Sexy High-Ticket Offer you'd like to sell at the end of your event?
- Decide what your event messaging will be. What is the name and promise of your event? Will this be a free or paid event? If it's paid, what's the ticket price?
- Decide on a date and time to do your event.

FILL UP

YOUR EVENT DOESN'T HAVE TO BE "FANCY" TO BE PROFITABLE

Filling your event with hundreds, even thousands of attendees is incredible. However, you don't need a big room to have a successful event.

Remember Amanda? She has a $100,000 weekend with 12 people in the room.

Now, I wanna tell you about Jessica.

Before hosting her first event, Jessica was looking to…

- Have more fun selling her offers
- Take less sales calls so she could spend more time with her family
- Sign clients without a call (speaking, in the DMs, and from content alone)

As soon as Jessica plugged into the Wealthy Woman Society, she started gaining massive momentum…

> **Jessica**
> This membership at such a small cost seriously gave me so much more momentum with the value in it then some things I've paid way more for. 🤍✨
> Anyone else feel the value inside is wildly massive for the price tag?

Within a few weeks, she launched and filled her first event, and when she made her very first invitation speaking to sell from her event… 40% of the room bought her high-ticket offer!

Jessica said, "It worked out better than I expected it to!"

Today, Jessica is working less, taking fewer sales calls, and making more money…

But more importantly, Jessica is able to focus on the things she loves to do, like creating content, giving back more, and spending time with her toddler and family. Jessica has been able to see extraordinary results because she shows up daily, moves at lightning speed, leans into the community for support, and implements feedback immediately inside the Wealthy Woman Society.

Oh… and the thing about Jessica's event? It was a potluck inside of a friend's store.

> **Jessica**
>
> Haven't posted in a bit so popping in just to share that I took a page from the book of Ally Kennedy and I made my own damn stage. 😊
>
> I couldn't find a local speaking op in May, so I made a small one in the form of a lunch and learn for local biz owners. 🍽️
>
> Hasn't even happened yet and people are already requesting more and asking more details about my offers. 👍

Before she even hosted the event, she had an influx of people inquiring about her offers. They saw Jessica lead. They saw Jessica was in The Wealth Zone. They saw Jessica as an Instant Influence Identity… and they felt, "I want to work with HER…"

I tell you this because your event doesn't need to be a huge production. Sure, those are fun. However, it gets easier. Your event can look however you want it to. Now that you have permission to launch your event your way, it's time to fill it.

YOU DON'T NEED A BIG AUDIENCE TO FILL YOUR EVENT.

"Thank you for posting about our event, Ally! There are over 20 comments so far!"

A huge smile lit up my face as I read a message from my VIP Event Consulting Clients. They were looking for guest speakers to help them fill their event. And if you're reading this chapter thinking, "Ally… I want to host an event, but I don't have a huge audience…" I'm going to show you a secret way to 2X-4X the number of attendees at your events without spending a dime on ads.

The best way to multiply the number of attendees at your events is using guest speakers.

Why does this work?

Speaking on stage is a huge desire for most entrepreneurs. And when you build your own stage? You have an asset most entrepreneurs are looking for. I like to say, "You're either the one building the stage, or the one applying to speak on it."

Plus, as humans, we have a desire to feel like we're a part of something bigger. When you mix that with the opportunity to build your brand, get noticed, build credibility, connect with potential clients... it's a no brainer.

Those 20 comments? Quickly turned into 196...

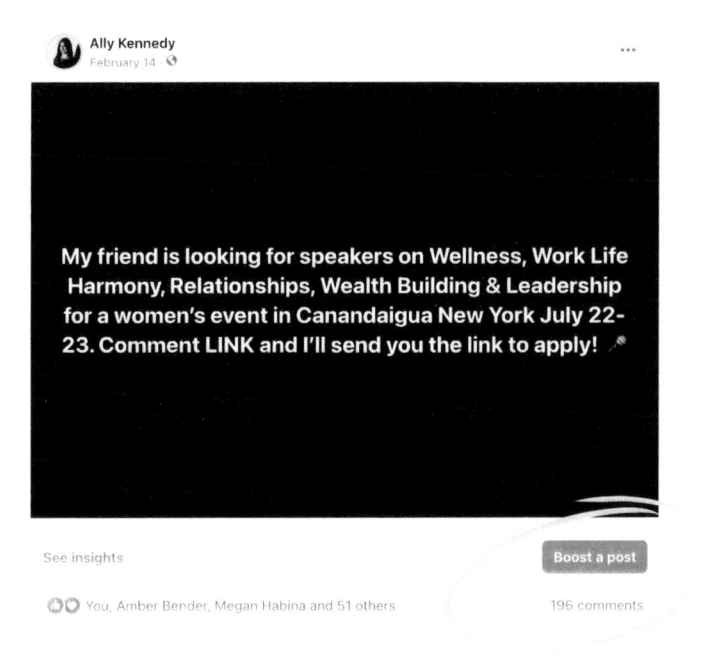

Ally Kennedy
February 14

My friend is looking for speakers on Wellness, Work Life Harmony, Relationships, Wealth Building & Leadership for a women's event in Canandaigua New York July 22-23. Comment LINK and I'll send you the link to apply!

See insights — Boost a post
You, Amber Bender, Megan Habina and 51 others — 196 comments

I recommend requiring your guest speakers to help you promote the event in exchange for promoting them to your audience. Book guest speakers who are in a complimentary niche, and are not teaching on the same topic as the offer you are selling. It's important to make it extremely clear that you will be the only one selling, and selling from your stage is not allowed.

Inside of **Six Figure Speaker**, we go deeper into the how-to of filing your event. You will receive playbooks that walk you through all of this step-by-step, including a 16-page playbook with three event strategies to fill your event for $0, a 7-Page Guest Speaker Packages workbook outlining the event mission, vision, requirements and boundaries, and a 12-page Marketing Swipe File for guest speakers to help promote your event.

Now that you've created your event and offer messaging, follow the steps below to launch and fill your event. In the next chapter, I'll show you what to say during your event to transform the lives of your attendees and get them excited to buy from you.

HOMEWORK

- Decide how you're going to fill your event
    - Email / Organic (your warmest audiences)
    - Bonus tickets to current (or past) clients and customers
    - Bonus tickets to paid programs that are converting when you sell it
    - Joint Venture (JV) with guest speakers who have an email list
    - Paid Traffic
    - Speaking Tour

- Launch your event to your list and following
    - Create Pre-Launch Strategy
    - Write Intro and Story Emails, FAQ Emails, Ticket Sales Emails, Client Case study emails
    - Take those emails and create social media posts out of them

- Upload them into your email service and send it to your list
- Publish on all platforms daily to promote
- Share social proof screenshots of people DMing you, opting in, etc.

• Post a Guest Speaker Handraiser Post
  - Do you know who's an expert in [INSERT TOPIC]? I'm looking for amazing guest speakers for an event!!! Please tag them in the comments

SHOW UP

ENGAGE AUDIENCES, CHANGE LIVES & GET SALES ON THE SPOT

Ever sit through a boring speaker? You're just, like, zoned out. Right? But when you watch a truly engaging, dynamic, powerful speaker? You will never forget it.

After traveling the country to train in person with the top sales speakers in the industry, doing $1Million and multi-million dollar days... What I've discovered is there's actually a formula for how they're doing that.

Yep. There's a framework. And if speakers don't use the framework?

It's boring.

When you do use the framework? The crowd goes wild. Standing, screaming, dancing, moving energy during your talk...

And at the end?

They're DMing you, inquiring about your programs, and buying like crazy. I recently showed this framework to my one on one In the Arena Speaker Training client. She was invited to speak on stage at an industry leader's conference. We worked one one one to craft her talk using this framework.

The result?

100% of the room inquired about her $20K offer after her 45 min talk... even though she wasn't allowed to sell or pitch her offer from stage. This is the same framework my clients use to sign 4-figure clients in as little as 15 minutes of speaking (without selling from stage or pitching her offer.)

When my clients do sell at the end of speaking using this framework? They sign five-figure clients within minutes of dropping an offer at events...collapsing their monthly income into a day. This is why I'm the secret weapon for seven-and eight-figure CEOs to consult on, speak, and sell from stage at their events.

Wealthy Women don't just speak to talk… they speak to make money every time they open their mouths.

Right now, you're making some money from your events, but you're not making insane money because you're uncertain how to engage the audience. You think, "I'll just get up and tell my story…easy!" So you start telling your story… What the audience hears? "I, I, I, me, me, me…"

It's kinda like when you meet a person at a party and they don't stop talking about themselves…You can start to see the audience's eyes glazing over. And it ends up being a boring lecture because you don't know how to turn your story into a two-way conversation that unleashes the energy of the audience.

During your presentation? You over teach and forget the most important piece of sales speaking… people buy when they feel like buying. Your job is to shift the way people feel because of your talk. When you do this right, you'll walk off the stage to payment notifications because your audience went to instagram to find your profile to FIND someone to buy from you… (even when you're not selling) because you made them FEEL like they need to be a part of your world.

And in this chapter, I'm going to teach you a simple framework from the Six Figure Speaker System, that you can implement right away, so you can speak in a way that has your DMs filled with inquiries from perfect fit clients (even when you're not "selling" from stage)…

First, you'll craft a Story Selling Structure that builds immediate certainty with your audience… positioning you and your offer as the obvious choice. Then, I'll show you how to seamlessly transition your content to the invitation to create more leads, sales, and inquiries from perfect fit clients.

Inside of *Speak Your Way to Wealth*, we're going to dive into Session 1 of your event, as I give you a taste of the Shape Your Signature Message Method. Inside of **Six Figure Speaker**, I walk you through this more in depth, in nine bite-sized modules, inducing the full 10-page Shape Your Signature Message Method Workbook.

When it comes to crafting content to speak to sell your high-ticket offers, the Shape Your Signature Message Method is the tip of the iceberg. However, the framework I'm about to teach you has helped our clients sign four-figure paid in full clients from 15 minutes of speaking.

Let's dive in.

HOW TO STRUCTURE YOUR EVENT CONTENT TO TURN ATTENDEES INTO CLIENTS

Before we dive into the Shape Your Signature Message Method, or "Session One" of your event, I want to show you how it fits into your overall event structure. Below is an overview of a 4-hour, or half day event structure. You can modify the structure into a two-day, three day event, up to a five day challenge, however, the principle will stay the same.

4 HOUR EVENT STRUCTURE

- VIP
- SESSION 1: SYSTEM ORIGIN STORY
- SESSION 2: THE SYSTEM
- SESSION 3: SYSTEM DEEP DIVE
- SESSION 4: SYSTEM DEEP DIVE
- SESSION 5: Q&A

Inside of *Speak You Way to Wealth*, we're going to focus on helping you Shape Your Signature message. By the end of this chapter, you'll craft a signature talk you can deliver at any length, from any platform, that is perfectly threaded to your Super Sexy High-Ticket Offer, so you can explode your business with clients saying "I'M IN!" & "How can I work with you?"

If you're looking for one on one support to Shape Your Signature Message, or launch your next virtual or in-person event, DM me on Instagram @theallykennedy for more information.

Shape Your Signature Message

The best presentations are 50% story and 50% strategy, activating the attendees to think bigger, move bigger, and adopt an identity that will support their success. Today, we'll begin to build out the structure of your talk. However, what amplifies your audiences' motivation to take action to join your offer, is when you layer in sales speaking techniques.

Inside of Six Figure Speaker, I break down the Fast Buyer Framework™, showing you how to get client signups on the spot for your high-ticket offers in as little as one event, without requiring a sales call. When you learn of these techniques you'll be 100% prepared to speak to sell from your own event or someone else's event.

For the full step-by-step curriculum, I recommend diving into Six Figure Speaker, which you get instant access to inside the Wealthy Woman Society. For now, let's Shape Your Signature Message, so you can ignite a new level of confidence & clarity in your message and turn your offer into a signature talk that gets you seen, known, and creates an influx of inbound DMS and payment notifications every time you speak from video, virtual event, podcast, or a stage.

SHAPE YOUR STORY

Step 1: Articulate the problem

What emotion(s) did you feel while you were experiencing the problem? Great speakers articulate emotions really well and take a minute to dimensionalize them. Speak to the internal AND external piece of each to do this.

We as humans connect more over pain than we do over pleasure. Make sure to articulate the pain you felt during the problem section of your story. What negative emotions is the audience currently feeling?

Have you experienced these emotions? I explain this in each step of the "how." I used the steps as the points I was facing major resistance, connected with my audience, and shared how I moved through it.

Example: They know they are meant for more (frustrated, uncomfortable), Already invested into every type of mentorship, don't know which direction to go (Uncertain), Are afraid to shift business model

Prompt: I was … [in this place], doing … [this thing]….and I felt … [like this]

Step 2: Articulate the solution

This is the moment that changed everything. The "aha" moment that led you to discovering the strategy. The solution usually happens when a guide appears. (mentor, coach, something you heard in a speech, book, ect). Suddenly, your whole life changed, when you (did this, heard this, read this, realized this ect.)

Prompt: All of a sudden, I [heard, read, went to an event, met this mentor, etc]…

Step 3: Articulate the Payoff

What happened after you implemented and discovered the strategy? Speak to the internal AND external payoffs. Get specific.

- What showed up in your life?
- More joy, clarity, confidence, money?
- What emotional internal things showed up?
- What external tangible results showed up?

Transition to strategy

Over the next [insert time fame] of implementing [the thing you found]... I discovered [insert headline of your talk / benefit you're going to teach] that I'm going to teach you over the next [#of minutes in your keynote.]

Action: Write out the story of how you found your strategy

SHAPE YOUR STRATEGY

Remember the Category of One Method you created in Part 2? This is what you're going to present in the strategy section of your Signature Message.

List the 3-4 steps to get from the problem to the solution. [This is the framework of your signature system / framework / blueprinting your offer]

Step 1
Step 2
Step 3
Step 4

Action: Write out the strategy portion of your signature message.

What case studies or social proof can you include from you or your clients to show that your strategy actually works?

Note: The framework of this piece of your talk will be structured like this...

Story
Strategy
Social proof

SHAPE YOUR INVITATION

To transition to the invitation, introduce this question into their mind...

So many of you are asking yourselves the questions, what next?

Action: Decide what you're going to offer for both scenarios of a free opt in and a paid offer at the end of your message.

Now it's time to get In the Arena and share your message! Sharing your Signature Message will skyrocket your leadership, authority & build trust with your audience at lightning speed, even if you don't have any experience as a speaker.

Before we get to your homework for this chapter, I want to show you what's possible when you share your Signature Message.

Here's what happened when Jenna shared her Signature Message for the first time, for 15 minutes virtually, with zero experience speaking...

HOW JENNA 4X'D HER PRICES IS ATTRACTING PAY-IN-FULL CLIENTS AND PAID SPEAKING OPPORTUNITIES FROM HER FIRST TIME ON STAGE

Work directly with me on your messaging and how you deliver it from a virtual or in-person stage, podcast, or even live video speaking to sell, and your business won't ever be the same.

Imagine signing four or five-figure clients every time you presented your signature talk from a virtual or in-person event because you decided to get the support you need speaking to sell?

Imagine getting known as the one in your industry who they can't take their eyes off of because you know how to command and engage a room so well that you started getting inbound speaking opportunities...

Imagine feeling confident that you don't have any gaps in your message and live presentation that would allow sales to slip through the cracks... even when you're not "pitching" from the stage?

That's exactly what happened when I worked with Jenna one on one on her Signature Message inside our Industry Icon Mastermind to deliver on stage at our quarterly summit. It was her first time speaking on stage. She had 15 minutes to present, and was not pitching her offer at the end of the presentation.

Before the event, she had a high-ticket, one-on-one offer she wanted to fill, and was talking about it on her Instagram stories for months. Sales were coming in for her other offers, but she had little traction on her one on one offer... so we worked 1:1 together to implement the Shape Your Signature Message Method to her talk, strategically leading to that offer without directly selling the offer onstage.

The result?

She signed her highest ticket, 1:1 clients, paid in full, at 4X her previous rate, from that 15 minute talk.

> Today I signed a 1:1 client into a 6 week human design coaching space with me!!! I'm so BEYOND FREAKING EXCITED! She's soul aligned, she's excited, she paid in full, just SO MANY WINS!!!

Within 20 days of speaking at our Wealthy Woman Summit, Jenna was…

- Attracting pay-in-full clients at 4X her original 1:1 rates
- Attracting paid speaking opportunities
- Igniting a new found power, confidence and certainty after taking the stage at our Wealthy Woman in-person and virtual events

Jenna's sales multiplied because she stepped into The Wealth Zone on that stage, and created an Instant Influence Identity in her brand.

Right now, your offers are incredible. Your work is life changing. It's not that your audience doesn't want to buy, does not see the value, or "can't afford" your offer… you just need to get into The Wealth Zone, and then deliver your message in a way that connects with your ideal clients and builds trust in a way that activates them to buy.

When you do this right, they trust you, your offer, and themselves to take action now.

You're letting sales slip through the cracks every time you show up to speak on camera, a livestream, a stage, or a virtual event by not working with me on your Signature Message.

HOW TO GET CLIENTS SAYING "I'M IN!!!" AND JOINING $20,000-$24,000 OFFERS WITHIN MINUTES OF DROPPING THEM

The Shape Your Signature Message Method will get you good results. But if you want insane results? If you want to see signups on the spot when you drop an offer from your event? You need to layer in the Fast Buyer Framework™. The Fast Buyer Framework™ is a checklist of 11 different sales speaking techniques to layer into your SIgnature Message and event content.

When you do this, people pull their credit cards out faster than you can say "Paid-in-full…" signing up for your offers on the spot at your events. The Fast Buyer Framework™ is the secret sauce that will have clients saying "I'M IN!!!" and joining even your highest ticket, $20,000+ offers within minutes of dropping them.

I break down the Fast Buyer Framework™ step-by-step inside of Six Figure Speaker, which you get immediate access to inside the Wealthy Woman Society.

HOMEWORK

- Go live and practice sharing your signature message. Invite your audience to join your offer at the end. Record a podcast episode doing the same. Practice this long form and in short form, like speaking on a reel (less than 90 seconds) or a single story slide (60 seconds). See how many different formats you can use to share your signature message. Use this to open a talk, event, livestream, presenting a unique piece of your method, to lead into an offer [free or paid], etc.

SELL OUT

MAXIMIZE POST-EVENT MOMENTUM AND SELL OUT YOUR OFFERS

Want to make more sales? The answer is simple. Sell more.

The Sell Out phase of your event launch is the most important phase of the SIx Figure Speaker System because you've built so much momentum.

The worst thing you can do here?

- Pull the plug
- Wobble and lower prices
- Decide to stop selling
- Slow down or stop before the finish line
- Quit your launch because you did not see a specific number of enrollments within a time period you made up in your head

And unfortunately, I see this too often when you don't get the instant validation of hitting a made up number on a made up timeline in your head.

Wealthy Women know that their success is not dependent on a single event. Wealthy Women play in decades. They know they will host hundreds of events and launches in their lifetime, so there is zero pressure on the performance of one single event.

That being said, to ensure you scoop up all the demand from the momentum you've built from your event...Inside of Six Figure Speaker (which is included when you enroll in the Wealthy Woman Society), I give you my exact 14-Days to Launch Trello Board System...

Including my Complete A to Z launch system, including done-for-you templates, checklists, automations, emails, frameworks, funnel steps, swipe files, templates... everything you need to launch and sell from virtual stage within the next 14 days.

I'm basically giving you a six-figure business. Templates are plug-and-play so you can simply swipe, customize, and deploy...Including my proven 4-step sales flows to get 10x more clients in your DMs, and the exact step-by-step DM framework I used to enroll $2,000-$20,000 clients in the DMs without a sales call.

In true Wealthy Woman style, it would be a disservice to you to just talk about the strategy of sales. Staying in The Wealth Zone during your Sell Out phase is what will determine your overall launch success. To help you stay inside The Wealth Zone during your launch, I'd love to share my beliefs around sales.

I encourage you to take these beliefs, of a modified version of them that lands for you, into your event launch, and take action in alignment with these beliefs daily.

Your money reality is a reflection of your decision to act in alignment with these beliefs daily… before you have the results—and without needing the results.

It is a decision to align your thoughts with what you want, not what has happened in the past.

So let's get you operating in alignment with someone who makes five and six figure cash days on *repeat*.

BELIEFS TO COLLAPSE YOUR MONTHLY INCOME INTO A DAY

- This will be my biggest launch ever and I'm going to make it happen. My audience loves everything I drop and they buy like CRAZY. I can't wait to sell today. I KNOW people will buy when I drop this. I KNOW people will sign up when I drop this.
- Today is going to be the BIGGEST day ever. Because why not? Anything is possible. My work is insane. It's possible for me to have bigger and bigger impact. It is possible for me to have bigger and bigger income.
- Five and six figure cash days are done. They are happening. They are my norm.

- My work is INSANELY valuable. The more people who experience my work, the better it is for them, the better it is for me, the better it is for everyone around them. My work is valuable and it would be CRAZY if people didn't say yes to it.
- People LOVE to buy from me, and people LOVE when I sell. It's fun and it's easy to sell. People love to pay. People love to buy. People love when I sell.
- Making money is easy, simple, and fun, and none of it needs to be complicated. Making it easy is a choice. Making it complicated is a choice. I choose to make money and sales easy.
- When I'm in The Wealth Zone, and I share my work in my power with the world, powerful people choose it for themselves. When I'm in The Wealth Zone, powerful people buy from me. Making money happens when power meets power.
- My job is to show up in my power and speak to sell my offers simply and powerfully. The more I show up, and speak to sell my offers, the more money I make.
- People buy every offer I drop. Everything sells effortlessly with the perfect clients when I'm convicted, and when I'm consistent. It's my job to be convicted and consistent. When I'm those two things, people buy everything I drop. It's a non negotiable. It's already happening. It's already done.
- More and more money flows to me when I focus on how much I love my work. When I let myself have fun. When I let myself enjoy the process. When I'm in flow. When I'm in The Wealth Zone. When I happily overdeliver, when I hold myself to a high standard, and when I lead myself, no matter what, more and more money always flows to me.
- People love to buy. My work is incredible. And I'm gonna stand for it no matter what. My offers are the hottest things on the internet streets.
- I know I am going to blow it up today and make insane sales. I know it. Because it's who I am and what I do. I am in control of my life, business, and income, and I'm gonna claim

it, own it, and be about it. I show up in my full conviction, knowingness, and power daily. No matter what.
- I know and I feel in my body that I am capable of getting paid five and six figures daily. It is possible for me. Of course that's what I do. Of course that amount of people buy from me.
- $100K cash is already on it's way to me. It's done. It's happening now. So… How do I show up? How do I post? Who do I choose to be because of it? How do I share my offer? What moves do I make? What prices do I have? What is my frequency? It's time to hold myself to this standard.

HOMEWORK

- Examine your current beliefs around sales. Are they supportive of the goals you have in your business?
- Examine your current daily actions around sales. What beliefs need to be strengthened so you can sell more consistently, and with more conviction?

LET TODAY BE THE DAY YOU LOOK BACK ON AS THE DAY THAT EVERYTHING CHANGED

I know what it's like to know you're meant for more…

And that's exactly why, in the next section, I'm going to give you an invitation to rise into your next level of leadership, income, and influence inside the Wealthy Woman Society.

As you approach the end of this book, you have two choices.

1) Stay where you are, and lay your head on your pillow every night knowing you've barely scratched the surface of what you're capable of…

2) Muster up the courage to say "YES" to yourself. To say "YES" to the level of impact you know you're meant to make. To say "YES" to a business model that is more powerful & leveraged… compounding so

you can create a life you're obsessed with, having so much more fun while making more and more money.

I know you read *Speak Your Way to Wealth* for a reason. I know what we've covered inside this book is exactly what you need. And I also know this will be a new edge for you... it will stretch you... But you can either stay in that fear, or you can decide to make a move today that changes everything.

And when you're ready to look back on today as the day that changed everything... I invite you to join us inside the Wealthy Woman Society to get my personalized support to implement the Wealthy Woman Way into your business.

In the next chapter, I'm going to break down what your life and business will look like on the other side of the Wealthy Woman Society.

IV: WEALTHY WOMAN SOCIETY

TAKE THE FAST LANE TO THE TOP OF YOUR INDUSTRY AND IMPLEMENT EVERYTHING YOU LEARNED IN A SINGLE WEEKEND

"In your mind, the sky isn't even the limit."
—Ally Kennedy

RIGHT NOW, YOU'RE ASKING YOURSELF, "WHAT'S NEXT?"

Reading a book is incredible, but unlocking exponential influence, impacting millions worldwide, and collapsing your monthly income into a day becomes a whole lot easier when you have the step-by-step curriculum, community, and personalized mentorship to plug in to daily...

And I want to give you the opportunity to plug in our community of women on the same mission to scale their impact, influence and offers as speakers inside the Wealthy Woman Society.

WEALTHY WOMAN Society

The **Wealthy Woman Society** is a 6 month mastermind for the ICONIC woman who wants to take the fast lane to the top of your industry, speak in a way that has your audience immediately think "I want to work with HER..."

And learn how to host events that impact thousands more around the globe and collapse your monthly income into a day.

But more importantly, **you'll BECOME the woman who people LOVE to buy high-ticket offers from.**

I created the Wealthy Woman Society to build a home for the pioneers, the disruptors, the innovators, the leaders of leaders, the bold women, becoming Industry Icons.

You see yourself becoming building a massive online business and speaking on stages and hosting events around the world...

You move at lightning speed… so fast most people can't keep up. You have a massive vision, so much bigger than *just* hitting an income milestone. In your mind, the sky isn't even the limit.

The Wealthy Woman Society is for you if…

- You know you're meant to multiply your income and impact online AND through speaking and hosting life-changing events … becoming wildly known as the obvious choice to hire… and you're ready to make that your reality
- You want to become the woman who continuously multiplies her income in every season of business and feels unshakable no matter how many sales are coming in or what number is in your bank account
- You want to elevate every piece of your brand and message to attract a higher-level client who won't bat an eyelash at even your highest prices, making sales feel as easy as breathing
- You're done being in rooms that are just talking about how to make five-figure months from social media. That's your bare minimum. You want to impact thousands more around the world speaking and hosting events. You're ready for a space that's normalizing five and six figures in a single day from events (even if you're not speaking and hosting events yet, you're ready to stretch yourself for the level of impact and income you're meant for.)

If you're ready to step into a new level of power, leadership, and spread your work like wildfire around the world, magnetizing your dream clients as a result…

I made the Wealthy Woman Society for you.

Inside, we'll focus on scaling your impact, influence, and offers the Wealthy Woman Way…

The Wealthy Woman Way to scaling your impact, influence and offers is to…

THE **WEALTHY WOMAN** WAY

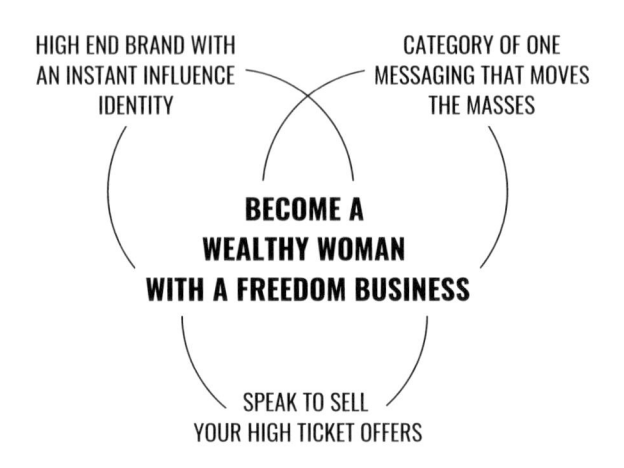

```
HIGH END BRAND WITH          CATEGORY OF ONE
AN INSTANT INFLUENCE         MESSAGING THAT MOVES
IDENTITY                     THE MASSES

            BECOME A
          WEALTHY WOMAN
      WITH A FREEDOM BUSINESS

              SPEAK TO SELL
          YOUR HIGH TICKET OFFERS
```

BUILD A HIGH END BRAND WITH AN INSTANT INFLUENCE IDENTITY

I want to teach you not only how to sell high-ticket offers, but how to become the woman who people love to buy high ticket from. If you're not signing clients into your highest ticket offers, it's not a messaging problem… it's a leadership or brand positioning problem.

CREATE CATEGORY OF ONE MESSAGING THAT MOVES THE MASSES

When you do this, you don't just stand out as the obvious choice in your industry… you are the industry. I'll teach you how to use Sensory Selling to speak or create content that makes dream clients think, "You're speaking to my soul" and pay in full. When you master creating Category of One messaging that moves the masses… You can fill your $2k–$20k+ offers from content alone…without sending 100 DMs or requiring a call.

SPEAK TO SELL YOUR HIGH-TICKET OFFERS

Speaking to sell is the #1 wealth building skill in the world. This is how you will collapse your monthly income into a day using your voice. When you master your messaging and speaking to sell, your current ceiling will become your new floor. Every part of your business will up level, conversion from every email, post, story, will compound into five and six figure days.

You will experience true freedom to sell what you want and live how you want, because you know how to speak to sell anything, your business is set up to create more leverage, and therefore, more space, and you have multiple streams of income coming in from your offers while getting paid to speak and travel.

If you are serious about blowing up your brand and business, you need to be inside the Wealthy Woman Society. DM me MASTERMIND on Instagram @theallykennedy to apply.

If you value speed, depth, and want my 1:1 support, want to multiply your influence, impact and see an extra 0 staring back at you at the end of your bank account even faster... I made the Wealthy Woman Society VIP Access Pass for you...

WEALTHY WOMAN *Society*
VIP ACCESS PASS

Wealthy Woman Society VIP Access Pass Includes the Wealthy Woman Society 6 Month Mastermind PLUS the following three experiences...

- Wealthy Woman Hotline 1:1 Telegram Experience
- Speak Your Way to Wealth Virtual VIP Day
- Wealthy Brand Immersion in San Diego, CA

The women who work with me inside of these three offers typically *make more money while doing less...* Because of the leverage we create through...

- Elevating your messaging to create more high-ticket buyers from content alone
- 1:1 event launch strategy to collapse their monthly income into a day
- Boutique, high end, done-for-you visual branding that creates an Instant Influence Identity that instantly makes dream clients feel "I want to work with HER..." without months of warming up

In the VIP Access Pass, we do more in a single day than six months in some coaching programs.

Here's everything you need to know about the Woman Society VIP Access Pass...

WEALTHY WOMAN *Hotline*

The Wealthy Woman Hotline is a 1:1 telegram experience with direct access to me for rapid-fire coaching and feedback, giving you access to the support & nuanced strategy that will stretch you into your next level of leadership, impact & income.

This is for you if you if...

- You want close proximity support and 1:1 personalized coaching with the exact leadership, identity & messaging shifts to break through to your next level of income

- You want to know the exact shifts to make to your messaging & sales strategies to multiply how many people join your offers
- You want a space to plug in that will help you remember who you are in the moments when you forget
- You feel you're on the verge of a massive breakthrough and you're ready to put yourself in a space that will support your next level.

WEALTHY SPEAKER *Vip Day*

The **Wealthy Speaker Vip Day** is a virtual VIP Day experience to craft your signature virtual or in-person event that will get you known around the world for your unique methodology.

You'll leave with the exact event blueprint (down to what to say & how to launch on the back end of your event to fill your offers) that you can rinse & repeat virtually or in person to sell out your high-ticket offers while impacting thousands more around the world, positioning you as an Industry Icon, & leaving attendees remembering your event as "the day that changed everything for them."

You'll learn to speak to sell your high-ticket offers in a way that has your attendees feel "I need to work with HER," effortlessly filling your $2,000-$20,000 programs as a byproduct.

This is for you if…

- You see yourself impacting thousands more speaking & facilitating… getting paid to speak on stages & host events or retreats around the world
- You want to host transformational events that impact thousands more through your work & speak in a way that has your DMs flooded with messages for weeks saying, "Your event changed my life…"

- You want to turn your body of work into a high-converting signature virtual or in-person event that fills your that fills your $2,000-$20,000 offers with dream clients
- You want to leave with the signature event & launch strategy mapped out that will support your highest cash launches in 2024 & beyond, setting you up to go into 2025 with 6-12 months of recurring revenue from your high-ticket offers
- You want a more leveraged business that leaves you feeling so fulfilled by the impact you're making... one that positions you to be paid to travel, speak from stages & host events around the world
- You're in a season of "how big and fast can I go?" You know speaking is your next step to exploding your influence, & 2X-ing, 4X-ing, even 10X-ing what you've already built.

DM me @theallykennedy on Instagram for more details to join the Wealthy Speaker VIP Day individually or inside the Wealthy Woman Society VIP Access Pass.

WEALTHY BRAND *Immersion*

The **Wealthy Brand Immersion** is a in-person VIP day & white glove experience in San Diego, CA, to elevate your brand to create a high end, Instant Influence Identity that attracts high paying clients without months of warming up.

In a single day, you'll shoot 3-6 months worth of video content to use to grow your social media & promote your signature high-ticket offers.

Imagine... arriving in San Diego, CA and checking into the iconic US Grant Hotel, known for hosting 15 U.S. Presidents, and countless Celebrities. You'll calibrate to your next level of Wealth the moment you step foot in the building.

You'll spend an entire day shooting with our production team, with me as your creative director, leaving with 3-6 months worth of video content to use to grow your social media audience & promote your signature high-ticket offers.

We'll also create one done-for-you promotional "movie trailer" video for your high-ticket signature offer that will position you as a Category of One... the obvious choice in your industry... so you can multiply the number of clients inside.

This is for you if...

- You're ready to elevate your brand identity & create a more premium positioning with quality assets that will build your brand for years to come
- You're in a season of raising your standards, boundaries & price points and you want your visual branding to reflect the growth you're experiencing as a leader & in your business
- You want to win the 50 millisecond sale, having people immediately feel "I need to be in her world..." the moment they find you & experience your brand
- You want your brand to feel more like a masterpiece that attracts quality clients who happily pay even your highest price points
- You know more people need to be inside your high-ticket spaces. You want your brand to visually communicate the immense power of your transformational work in a way that canvas graphics & words simply cannot.

DM me @theallykennedy on Instagram for more details to join the Wealthy Brand Immersion individually or inside the Wealthy Woman Society VIP Access Pass.

WEALTHY WOMAN *Society*
VIP ACCESS PASS

This is your opportunity to join the Wealthy Woman Society at an elevated level—one that gives you the support, strategy, and access to help you achieve Icon status in your Industry, multiply your impact, and achieve your biggest money goals in the process.

The VIP ACCESS PASS is for you if:

- You're *not* the kind of person who does anything basic. You are an Iconic woman, and you want your brand & business to reflect that.
- You want my eyes on your brand, messaging & business so you know exactly what to shift to impact thousands more & multiply the number of people in your paid offers.
- You want to see thousands more come in each month from elevating your brand, messaging & the way you speak about your offers to make attracting clients into your high level mentorship spaces feel as easy as breathing
- You know you're on the verge of a massive up-level, you're meant to be KNOWN in your industry, and you're ready for hands-on support to make it happen.
- You've been wanting to work with me in close proximity & get in the room with other Industry Icons and now feels like the perfect time.

If the Wealthy Woman Society, the VIP Access Pass, or access to one of these exclusive experiences on their own is speaking to you...

DM me on Instagram @theallykennedy to apply for the Wealthy Woman Society, Join the VIP access Pass, or jump into a single experience.

MAKING SALES ON SOCIAL MEDIA AND MAKING SALES SPEAKING TO SELL ARE TWO ENTIRELY DIFFERENT WORLDS

It takes a very different set of skills to create multi 5-figures, or 6-figures in a month than it does to create multi 5, or 6- figures in a single day.

I'm the mentor you hire when you want to host events that impact thousands more around the globe AND collapse your monthly income into a day.

When you're ready to host events that convert to high paying clients who enroll on the spot from your events... You can't afford *not* to work with me.

And there's never been a better time to join the Wealthy Woman Movement.

When you're ready for a home that will activate you...Give you the nuanced, personalized strategy to grow your online business...

AND bring your message to the world in a much BIGGER way, speaking & hosting events... so you can get KNOWN in your industry, impact thousands more around the globe, and 2X-5X your income...

You need to be inside the Wealthy Woman Society. DM me on Instagram @theallykennedy to apply.You're one DM away from entering a world that has everything you need to blow up your business, impact thousands more through your life changing work & create an industry of your own.

XO
Ally

YOUR NEXT STEPS

"You don't exist inside of an industry. You are the industry."
—Ally Kennedy

JOIN THE WEALTHY SPEAKER SOCIETY 6 MONTH MASTERMIND

The Wealthy Woman Society is a 6 month mastermind for the ICONIC woman who wants to take the fast lane to the top of your industry, speak in a way that has your audience immediately think "I want to work with HER..."

And learn how to host events that impact thousands more around the globe & collapse your monthly income into a day.

But more importantly, you'll BECOME the woman who people LOVE to buy high ticket from.

WHAT'S INCLUDED?

Once you're accepted you'll have immediate access to...

- 1:1 Private Onboarding & Planning Call
- Six Figure Speaker ($1997 value)

The Wealthy Woman Society is designed to help you spark & ignite momentum with...

- 2X Monthly calls
- Weekly plug-in with me in to map out your sales & content strategy
- Private Mastermind community chat
- 1:1 Quarterly Planning
- Quarterly Mastermind Session

During your six months of mentorship you will have biweekly mentorship calls where you get hands-on feedback on your Category of One messaging, event launch, and sales strategy. This is priceless. The ability to have someone who can workshop copy with you to sell your offers can 10X your business in half the time.

You will be in a Telegram group with everyone else who has decided that these next six months are going to be the BEST six months of their life. You get a weekly mastermind day in Telegram with Ally to get personalized support and ask questions. Outside of mastermind days, you will be able to workshop with the women inside of the Wealthy Woman Society.

You get immediate access to the Six Figure Speaker Program to learn how to launch events that collapse your monthly income into a day, make more sales speaking, and get KNOWN around the world for what you teach. You will embody energetics that make you feel unshakable in every season of business, no matter how many sales are coming in or what number is in your bank account.

DM me on Instagram @theallykennedy to apply to the Wealthy Woman Society.

V: WEALTHY SPEAKER WORKSHOP

ACCESS YOUR COMPLIMENTARY TICKET TO THE WEALTHY SPEAKER WORKSHOP

WEALTHY SPEAKER *Workshop*

ACCESS YOUR COMPLIMENTARY TICKET TO THE WEALTHY SPEAKER WORKSHOP

Implement what you've learned inside of Speak Your Way to Wealth inside of the Wealthy Speaker Workshop. Inside, you'll shape a message that's a match for millions to deliver in your own virtual or in-person event, or to share from stages around the world, so you can multiply your impact, collapse your monthly income into a day, and become internationally known for your expertise.